Milica Vladova

GLUTEN FREE COOKING

Gluten Free Baking, Wheat Free Bread Recipes, Celiac Disease Meals, Veganish and Ketogenic Diet Snacks, Souping Ideas, Vegetable Muffin Tin Recipes, and more

Milica Vladova
"Gluten Free Cooking: Gluten Free Baking, Wheat Free Bread Recipes, Celiac Disease Meals, Veganish and Ketogenic Diet Snacks, Souping Ideas, Vegetable Muffin Tin Recipes, and more"

Copyright © 2018 by Militsa Vladova

All rights reserved.

No part of this book may be reproduced in any form or by any electronic or mechanical means including information storage and retrieval systems, without permission in writing from the author. The only exception is by a reviewer, who may quote short excerpts in a review.

For permission requests, contact the author at www.mindbodyandspiritwellbeing.com.

The author and the publisher are in no way liable for any misuse of the material.

This book is not intended as a substitute for the medical advice of physicians. The reader should regularly consult a physician in matters relating to his/her health and particularly with respect to any symptoms that may require diagnosis or medical attention. The information I share in this book is based on my personal experience, conclusions, observations and studies. I am not a medical professional, nor a health expert. Before implementing any of the information shared in this book, consult with your physician or nutritionist! No information in this book should be used to diagnose, treat, prevent or cure any disease or condition.By reading this book, you acknowledge that you are responsible for your own health decisions. Do not take anything from this book and try it without proper research and medical supervision. The author does not assume any responsibility for any injuries or accidents.

FREE EBOOKS

Strengthen your immunity, detox, energize, heal, and stimulate your metabolism with these magical potent healthy recipes!

Get your FREE copy of
"*10 Powerful Immune Boosting Recipes*"
"*12 Healthy Dessert Recipes*"
"*15 Delicious & Healthy Smoothies*"
"*The Complete Ayurveda Detox*"

Go to **www.MindBodyAndSpiritWellbeing.com** and claim your book!

Or simply scan the QR code below:

Dedicated to all the people battling with chronic diseases every single day!

You are true heroes!

Contents

FREE EBOOKS 5

Introduction 15

GLUTEN-FREE BREAD AND BUNS 19

    Simple Pita Bread 21

    Tomato Pita Bread (Vegan) 22

    Sesame Tahini Bread (Low Carb) 23

    Quinoa Bread 24

    Dairy-free Bread 25

    Simple Bread 26

    Gluten-free Bread 27

    Gluten-free Bread with Eggs (Low Carb) 28

    Almond Bread with Chia 29

    Very Simple Bread with Tapioca 30

    Corn Bread I 31

    Corn Bread II 32

    French Cassava Bread (Paleo) 33

    Mozzarella Corn Bread 34

    Chickpea Falafel Bread (Vegan) 36

    Chickpea Bread 38

    Protein Bread I 39

    Protein Bread II 40

Cabbage Bread 41

Tasty Bread with Seeds and Veggies 43

Pea Bread with Stinging Nettle 44

Fast and Easy Pita Bread 46

Bread with Cream Cheese 47

Easy Bread (for Home Bread Machine) I 48

Easy Bread (for Home Bread Machine) II 49

Brazilian Bread Buns 50

Vegetable Bread Buns 51

Fast & Easy Bread Bites (Low Carb) 52

Zucchini Bread Bites (Low Carb) 53

Gluten-free Buns 54

Spinach Buns 56

Gluten-free Fiber Hamburger Buns 58

Quick Hamburger Bun in a Cup 59

Guilt-free Hamburger Buns (Low Carb) 60

2-Ingredient Potato Pancakes (Vegan) 61

Green Pancakes 62

GLUTEN-FREE PIZZA 63

Low Crab Gluten-free Pizza Crust (with Extra Fiber) 65

Vegan Gluten-free Pizza Crust 66

Corn Pizza Crust 67

Mini Pizza Crusts (Vegan) 68

Red Lentil Pizza Crust (Vegan) 69

Quinoa Pizza Crust 70

Eggplant Pizzas (Low Carb) 71

Zucchini Pizza (Low Carb) 72

Omelette Pizza 73

GLUTEN-FREE PASTRIES FROM THE BALKANS 75

Gluten-free Pita I 77

Gluten-free Pita II 78

Gluten-free Burek (Banitsa) I 79

Gluten-free Burek (Banitsa) II 80

Easy Gluten-free Spanakopita 81

Lazy Spanakopita with Feta Cheese 82

Lazy Winter Burek with Leek 84

Rice Banitsa Rolls 85

Leek and Mushroom Banitsa Rolls 86

Rice Balkan Burek (Tutmanik) 88

Tutmanik with Yellow Cheese 89

Fast and Easy Balkan Bureks on a Skillet 90

Salty Cake with Blue Cheese 91

Salty Cake with Zucchini 92

Cauliflower and Batata Quiche 93

Turkish Leafy Green Pancakes (Kaygana) 94

GLUTEN-FREE SNACKS AND BITES 95

Very Easy Cheesy Bites (Low Carb) 97

Puffy Cheesy Bites 98

Cheese Balls with Corn 99

Parsley Balls with White Sauce 100

Vegetable Rissoles 101

Salty Snacks with Walnuts 103

Corn Snacks with Cheese 104

Gluten-free Bake Rolls 105

Gluten-free Salty Snacks 106

Gluten-free Salty Snacks with Lard 107

Homemade Nachos 108

    Homemade Avocado Mayonnaise 110

    Homemade Avocado Mayonnaise (Vegan) 111

Very Simple Salty Sticks 112

Salty Corn Sticks 113

GLUTEN-FREE MUFFINS 115

Salty Muffins I 117

Salty Muffins II (with Feta Cheese) 118

Salty Muffins III 119

Salty Muffins IV (with Cream Cheese) 120

Salty Muffins V (with Powerful Healing Spices) 121

Vegetable Muffins 122

Muffins with Cream Cheese and Zucchinis (Low Carb) 123

Potato Muffins ... 124

Egg Muffins with Mushrooms (Low Carb) ... 125

OTHER GLUTEN-FREE MEALS AND SIDE DISHES ... 127

Stuffed Peppers with Buckwheat ... 129

Stuffed Zucchini with Onion Sauce ... 130

Vegetable Casserole ... 131

Chickpea "Meatballs" ... 133

Chicken Meatballs ... 134

Meatballs with Tartar Sauce (Low Carb) ... 135

Quinoa "Risotto" ... 136

Imperial Lunch ... 138

"Risotto" With Eggs ... 139

Cauliflower Moussaka ... 140

Zucchini "Pasta" with Bolognese Sauce (Low Carb) ... 142

Summer Zucchini Frittata (Low Carb) ... 144

Mini Veggie Muffin Omelettes (Low Carb) ... 145

Cream Cheese Omelette (Low Carb) ... 146

Zucchini & Chicken Rolls (Low Carb) ... 147

Zucchini & Cheese Rolls (Low Carb) ... 148

Zucchini & Cream Cheese Roll (Low Carb) ... 149

Rhodopean Potato Dish (Patatnik) ... 150

Stuffed Potatoes with Bacon ... 151

Stuffed Pumpkin with Meat ... 153

Vegan Romanian Polenta (Mamaliga) 154

Gluten-free Gypsy Schnitzel 155

Gourmet Appetizer with Salmon, Lentils, and Quinoa 157

Chestnut & Squash Cream Soup 160

Vegetable Cream Soup with Croutons 161

Mangold Soup (Vegan) 163

Summer Russian Soup (Okroshka) 164

Low Carb Summer Bulgarian Soup with Radish (Tarator) 165

Red Lentil Pate (Vegan) 166

Thank you! 167

About the author 168

Introduction

In book 1 of the Gluten Free Cookbook Series, "Easy Gluten Free Desserts", we have explored why it is so important to stay away from gluten, even if you do not have such food sensitivity!

Now, we are going to focus on the positives – how the gluten-free lifestyle can benefit our health and overall wellbeing!

The gluten-free diet benefits can be numerous. Logically, when we exclude this allergy-causing protein from our meals, we can expect to see huge improvements in our health and wellness.

What can we expect from eliminating gluten? I can tell you first hand that the gluten-free diet has been a real blessing for me. A lot of my long-term health issues were resolved by making that one simple change in my diet.

Take a look at my favorite gluten-free diet benefits I experienced quickly after taking this leap!

➢ Less bloating (relieving the IBS symptoms)

As I have mentioned in the previous book, gluten has been responsible for my constant bloating, meteorism, and severe IBS discomforts. And logically, right after ditching this wheat protein, the pain stopped – so quickly and so magically that it seemed too good to be true! So, if you suffer from any of these unpleasant discomforts, try to be gluten-free for a while and see if this was the root of the problem!

> **Clearer mind and better mood**

Gluten can really mess up your biochemistry and cause brain fog, difficulty concentrating, ADHD, even depression, and anxiety.

As soon as I decreased my gluten intake, I was feeling significantly better with regards to my mental health and emotional state. I was feeling much more clear-minded with fewer and fewer mood swings. For a person like me, who has been through severe psycho-somatic depression, taking care of my mental health is a top priority! I pay attention to anything that might trigger this ailment and try to eradicate it from my lifestyle ASAP! So, if you have any episodes of anxiety or depression (even the mildest!), seriously consider eliminating gluten from your diet!

> **Weight loss**

Although the link between gluten and weight gain is a little bit indirect, there is still a correlation. And the logic behind it is this – most foods which contain this protein are also rich in carbohydrates (like bread and pastries). And carbs are notorious for elevating the blood sugar levels and subsequently – the insulin hormone secretion. Insulin, on the other hand, is also known as the "fat storage hormone" – it is responsible for preparing our bodies for possible future food shortages. But these caloric deficits may never come (as it usually happens), and the results are rather scaring – the weight keeps piling up, and the cardiovascular system gets more and more overloaded.

When switching to gluten-free foods, most people experience a natural and healthy weight-loss because the intake of carbohydrates is limited. And as a consequence –

the insulin rushes are far fewer and the weight gain is restricted.

And this is not just an empty theory – many people have seen this beneficial side effect through their own experience and empirical evidence.

So, should you have any issues with your weight, try going gluten-free and focusing on the low carb substitutes of the regular wheat (like flax seed flour, coconut flour, almond flour, etc.).

> ### Less inflammation

One of the best gluten-free diet benefits is reducing the inflammation in our bodies. As we have learned previously, consuming a lot of gluten irritates the intestinal walls, causing micro wounds to the mucosa. As a result – our system reacts and tries to heal this tissue which elevates the temperature of this area and it becomes inflamed. If this occurs in a short-term manner, the body can easily manage the situation. But think about what happens when we continuously irritate the guts and create more and more of these small (but dangerous) slashes. That's right – the inflammation becomes chronic, more difficult to treat, and, sadly – it starts to spread all over the body in the form of arthritic pain, allergies, food intolerances, skin ailments, etc.

So, the first step towards the recovery from any form of inflammation could be getting rid of gluten, even if this means being on a gluten-free diet for a set period of time. If you have any issues with such health problems, definitely try the gluten-free lifestyle!

> **More energy**

As I have mentioned before, most gluten-rich foods are packed with carbohydrates. And these carbs create a vicious cycle of blood sugar surges and insulin spikes. What happens when the initial energy boost we get from the sugar intake fades away, is a sudden drop in our energetic levels. We get sleepy, sluggish, and even moody.

On the flip side, if we cut our consumption of carbohydrates, our energy levels stay stable throughout the day, and we feel more vital, calm, and clear-minded. So, in case you have any troubles with your productivity during the day, make sure you substitute your gluten foods with their low carb alternatives. For example, almond flour, coconut flour, flax seed flour, stevia, etc. This is one of the best combos – you heal your guts, shred some extra fat, and keep a stable high energy level for long hours!

I hope now you can see all of the wonderful benefits of going gluten-free! Although this is not intended to be the full list of positives from getting rid of this wheat protein, it still points out most of the common problems people struggle with on a daily basis.

So, bottom line is – test this out! If you wish to see if these effects will be true for you – just try and observe the results! And you may be surprised!

And now, let's get to the recipes! I hope you get a ton of ideas how to incorporate the gluten-free meals in your lifestyle and ultimately, improve your health and energy level!

Let's cook!

GLUTEN-FREE BREAD AND BUNS

Simple Pita Bread

Ingredients:

2 **Eggs**
1 cup **Yogurt**
1/2 tsp. **Baking soda**
1/2 cup **Kefir**
1/2 cup **Cream cheese spread**
2 Tbsps. **Butter**
A pinch of **Salt**
1 1/2 cup **Rice flour**
1/2 cup **Feta cheese**
Some **Olives** (pitted)
1/2 cup **Bacon**

Instructions:

First, mix the yogurt with the baking soda and leave the dairy product to froth for a bit.

In the meantime, cut the olives in slices, dice the bacon, and mash the feta cheese into crumbs.

At the point, you can start heating the oven to 200° C/ 392° F.

Next, combine all main ingredients (eggs, yogurt, kefir, cream cheese, butter, salt, rice flour) in a large bowl and blend them with a hand mixer.

Finally, add the mashed cheese, the olives, the bacon pieces, and stir nicely with a spoon.

Pour the mixture in a baking pan (about 10" x 15") covered with baking paper, and bake in the pre-heated oven until fully cooked.

Make sure you check with a wooden toothpick if the pita is well baked.

Tomato Pita Bread (Vegan)

Ingredients:

4 cups **Tomatoes** (diced)
A fistful of **Olives** (pitted)
1 **Red onion bulb**
Some **Garlic** – to taste
Spices – **oregano, basil, salt, pepper, turmeric**, etc. – to taste
2-3 Tbsps. **Olive oil**
4 Tbsps. **Gluten-free flour of choice**

Instructions:

This recipe is also very fast and easy, so you can start by heating the oven to 200° C/ 392° F.

Next, slice the olives and mix them with the tomato cubes.

Consecutively, simply add the remaining ingredients and stir well to blend them completely.

Now take a flat baking tray and cover it with parchment paper.

Transfer the pita mixture in the container and bake for about 40 minutes.

And that's it!

I know this awesome meal smells awesome, but wait for it to cool down completely before consuming!

Sesame Tahini Bread (Low Carb)

Ingredients:

1 1/2 cup **Sesame tahini**
4 **Eggs**
1 tsp. **Baking soda**
1 Tbsp. **Lemon juice**
1/2 cup **Water**
Salt and spices – to taste

Instructions:

Start heating the oven to 180° C/ 356° F.

Next, mix the baking soda with the lemon juice, and wait for the chemical reaction to subside.

In the meantime, beat the eggs and mix them with the tahini.

Next, add the lemon juice with the baking soda and start blending the mixture with a hand mixer or a blender.

Start slowly adding the water as you continue to blend the dough.

Add more water, if needed to reach the consistency of a typical cake batter – not too thick, not too runny.

Add the spices and stir again.

Pour the mixture in a baking mold (about 7" x 4") and cook until fully baked (about 35 minutes).

Quinoa Bread

Ingredients:

1 cup **Quinoa**
1 cup **Wholegrain basmati rice**
2 Tbsps. **Butter**
1 cup **Yogurt**
4 **Eggs**
1/2 tsp. **Baking soda**
Salt and oregano – to taste
1/2 tsp. **Lemon juice**

Instructions:

This recipe requires a little bit of prep work beforehand!

So, start the day before by washing and soaking the quinoa and the rice in some clean water.

The next morning, strain the grains and wash them thoroughly once again with water.

Leave the rice to dry out completely and grind it in a kitchen chopper or a coffee grinder.

Next, mix the baking soda and the lemon juice with the yogurt and let it froth for a bit.

Consecutively, mix all ingredients in a blender (or other suitable utensil like a kitchen chopper or a robot) and mince until the mixture becomes homogeneous.

Now you can start heating the oven to 180° C/ 356° F.

In the meantime, take a baking mold and cover it with baking paper.

Pour the batter in and bake the bread for about one hour until fully cooked.

Leave the dish to cool down completely before consuming. It is best to leave it aside overnight to enhance its taste!

Dairy-free Bread

Ingredients:

3 **Eggs**
1/2 tsp. **Salt**
1/3 cup **Olive oil**
1/2 tsp. **Baking soda**
1/2 tsp. **Apple cider vinegar**
1/2 cup **Ground almonds**
1/2 cup **Water**
2 1/2 Tbsps. **Millet flour**
2 1/2 Tbsps. **Rosehip flour**
2 Tbsps. **Poppy seeds**
1 Tbsp. **Sesame seeds**
1 Tbsp. **Flax seeds** (ground)
Some **Butter**

Instructions:

You can start by heating the oven to 180° C/ 356° F.

Next, beat the eggs in a large bowl.

Consecutively, mix the baking soda with the vinegar and wait for the chemical reaction to subside.

Next, add the sour mixture to the eggs and blend with a hand mixer.

Continue to add every single ingredient (except the butter) while continuing to stir.

You should get a nice homogeneous thick consistency like cake mixture.

Next, take a suitable bread baking mold and grease it with the butter.

Pour the batter in and bake for about 30 minutes (until fully cooked).

When the bread is ready, take it off the mold and wrap it in a towel to cool down completely.

Simple Bread

Ingredients:

1/2 cup **Rice flour**
1/2 cup **Chickpea flour**
1/2 cup **Corn starch** (non-GMO)
1/2 cup **Tapioca starch**
1 tsp. **Baking soda**
1/2 cup **Yogurt**

Instructions:

First, you can start heating the oven to 200° C/ 392° F.

Mix the yogurt with the baking soda and let it form bubbles.

Next, mix all the flours in a large bowl and blend them well.

After that, add the bubbly yogurt and stir nicely with a wooden spoon.

When the mixture is completely homogenized, we are ready for the final part.

Take a suitable bread baking mold and cover it parchment paper.

Pour the mixture in and bake for about 20-30 minutes (until the toothpick comes out clean). If your oven is fan-assisted, switch on the fan.

When the bread is fully cooked, take it out, wrap it in a clean kitchen towel, and leave it to cool down completely before consuming.

Gluten-free Bread

Ingredients:

1 cup **Corn flour** (non-GMO)
1 cup **Rice flour**
1/2 cup **Chickpea flour**
1/2 cup **Millet flour**
2 cups **Yogurt**
1 tsp. **Baking soda**
1 tsp. **Apple cider vinegar** (ACV)
2 **Eggs**
1 Tbsp. **Olive oil**
1 tsp. **Salt** (ground sea salt or Himalayan)
2 Tbsps. **Pumpkin seeds**

Instructions:

Mix the yogurt with the baking soda and the vinegar in a large bowl and blend them well.

Leave the mixture to froth for a bit.

Next, simply add the remaining ingredients and blend again. You can use a hand mixer to make the process easier.

Heat the oven to 180° C/ 356° F and bake the bread for 40 minutes.

Finally, cover the dish with baking paper and cook for 20-25 more minutes.

When the bread is ready, take it out of the baking pan and leave it to cool down on a grid wrapped in a kitchen towel.

Gluten-free Bread with Eggs (Low Carb)

Ingredients:

1/2 cup **Coconut flour**
6 medium **Eggs**
5-6 Tbsps. **Butter** (melted)
1 1/2 cup **Sour cream**
Spices (garlic powder, Rosemary, etc.) – to taste

Instructions:

Beat the eggs in a bowl and blend them with the remaining ingredients.

The consistency should be similar to cake batter.

Start heating the oven to 180° C/ 356° F.

Pour the mixture in a bread mold and bake until fully cooked.

Check with a toothpick if the pastry is ready!

Almond Bread with Chia

Ingredients:

2 cups **Almond flour**
2/3 cup **Tapioca flour**
2 Tbsps. **Ground flax seeds**
1 Tbsp. **Chia seeds**
1 tsp. **Baking soda**
A pinch of **Salt**
3 **Eggs**
1/4 cup **Coconut milk**
1 Tbsp. **Maple syrup**
1/4 cup **Coconut butter**
1 tsp. **Apple cider vinegar**

Instructions:

Start by heating the oven to 180° C/ 356° F.

Next, mix the dry ingredients in a bowl, and the liquid components - in another container.

Now gently and slowly start blending both mixtures until fully homogeneous.

Take a baking mold and cover it with baking paper.

Pour the batter in and bake for about 30-40 minutes (until golden and when the toothpick comes out clean).

Very Simple Bread with Tapioca

Ingredients:

6 Tbsps. (heaped) **Rice flour**
2 Tbsps. (heaped) **Corn flour** (non-GMO)
3 Tbsps. **Tapioca starch**
4 Tbsps. **Gluten-free flour mix**
A pinch of **Salt**
1/2 tsp. **Gluten-free yeast**
2 Tbsps. **Olive oil**
1 cup **Water**

Instructions:

Simply blend all ingredients and leave the dough to rise for about an hour.

Now heat the oven to 180° C/ 356° F and bake in a suitable bread baking mold for about 50 minutes.

And that's it!

My notes:

Corn Bread I

Ingredients:

4 **Eggs**
2 cups **Yogurt**
1 tsp. **Baking soda**
1 cup **Feta cheese**
3 cups **Corn flour** (non-GMO)
3 Tbsps. **Olive oil**
Savory – to taste

Instructions:

First, mix the yogurt with the baking soda and stir.

While the yogurt is reacting with the soda, beat the eggs in a large bowl.

Next, add all the remaining ingredients and blend well.

Transfer the mixture in a baking pan covered with parchment paper. Alternatively, you can grease the pan with some butter, olive oil, etc.

Heat the oven to 200° C/ 392° F and bake until fully cooked.

Finally, remove the hot bread from the pan and wrap it in a clean kitchen towel to cool down.

Corn Bread II

Ingredients:

2 **Eggs**
1 cup **Yogurt**
1 tsp. **Baking soda**
1/2 cup **Rice flour**
1 1/2 cup **Corn flour** (non-GMO)
3 Tbsps. **Olive oil**
Some **Water**

Instructions:

Start by mixing the yogurt with the baking soda and leave it to froth for a bit.

Next, beat the eggs in a bowl and mix them with the bubbly yogurt, the rice flour, the corn flour, and the olive oil.

Stir and blend the mixture to break down any lumps and homogenize it completely.

Now add some water until you reach the consistency of thick cake batter.

Turn on the oven at 180° C/ 356° F and bake the bread in your favorite baking mold for about 30 minutes (or until fully cooked and golden). You know, all ovens behave differently! ☺

French Cassava Bread (Paleo)

Ingredients:

1/2 cup **Water**
4 cups **Cassava flour**
4 **Eggs**
2 tsps. **Yeast**
2 Tbsps. **Honey**
1 Tbsp. **Salt**
3-4 Tbsps. **Olive oil**

Instructions:

First, separate the egg yolks from the whites.

Next, place the water in a large bowl, and mix it with the honey, the egg yolks, the olive oil, and the yeast.

In another container, whisk the egg whites until stiff. Use a hand mixer, if you wish to make the process easier.

Now, take half of the cassava flour and mix it with the salt.

Transfer to the main mixture, and add the egg whites as well.

Stir and blend as you start slowly adding the remaining of the flour.

The goal is to have homogeneous thick dough.

Place the bread in a baking pan, greased with some oil or butter.

Shape it in the desired form and make cuts along the dough.

Heat the oven to 190° C/ 374° F and bake for about 35 minutes. Voila!

Mozzarella Corn Bread

Ingredients:

For the dough:
1 cup **Warm water**
1 1/2 tsp. **Yeast** (dry)
1/2 cup **Corn flour** (non-GMO)
1 cup **Gluten-free flour mix**
1 tsp. **Muscovado sugar**
2 tsps. **Salt**
4 Tbsps. **Olive oil**

For the filling:
1/2 cup **Mozzarella**
4 **Dried tomatoes** (marinated in oil)
2 cloves **Garlic**
1/3 bunch **Parsley**
3 Tbsps. **Olive oil** (or the oil from the tomatoes)
3 Tbsps. **Pesto Genovese**
10 **Olives** (pitted)

Instructions:

Start by mixing the warm water, the yeast, sugar, and 1/2 cup of the gluten-free flour mix in a suitable container.

Stir well and leave the mixture to froth for a couple of hours or overnight. The point is to prepare fermented flour (kvass) which is much healthier for the intestines and easier to digest!

Next, add the salt, olive oil, the corn flour, and the remaining of the flour mix.

Start stirring and blending until you reach soft and pliable dough.

Continue kneading the mixture for about 6-7 more minutes.

Consecutively, leave the dough to rise until it doubles its size.

In the meantime, we can start preparing the filling.

Remove the stems from the parsley stalks and cut the green leaves in small pieces.

Dice the mozzarella, the olives, the marinated tomatoes, and the garlic cloves as well.

Mix the ingredients well along with the pesto and the olive oil.

Stir and blend the mixture well.

Now it is time to assemble the bread.

Transfer the dough on a kitchen counter covered with flour (gluten-free).

Roll it out to about half a centimeter width.

Next, spread the filling on top to cover the whole space.

After that, cut the bread sheet in thin stripes (about 3 cm/1 inch). Use a pizza cutter, if you have one.

Take a baking pan with approximately 9 inch diameter and cover it with baking paper.

Now roll each bread strip with the shape of a small rose. Place all roses in the baking pan tightly side by side.

Leave the bread to rise once more for about 20-30 minutes.

Meanwhile, heat the oven to 200° C/ 392° F.

Bake this deliciousness for about 30 minutes until fully cooked and golden.

Bon appetite!

Chickpea Falafel Bread (Vegan)

Ingredients:

For the hummus:
1 1/2 cup **Chickpeas** (boiled or canned)
3 Tbsps. **Sesame tahini**
3 cloves **Garlic**
1/2 cup **Water**
A pinch of **Salt**
2-3 Tbsps. **Olive oil**

For the bread:
1/2 cup **Olives** (pitted)
Some **Fresh parsley** – to taste
Some **Spices of choice** (pepper, curry, cumin, paprika) – to taste
3 cups **Chickpea flour**
2 tsps. **Baking powder**
A pinch of **Salt**
1 tsp. **Pectin**
1 Tbsp. **Sesame tahini**
Some **Sunflower seeds** – for decoration
Some **Water** - optional

Instructions:

First, we need to prepare the hummus.
Place the ingredients (chickpeas, olive oil, garlic, water, and salt) in a kitchen chopper or a robot. Mince them well to homogenize the mixture. If you wish to make it

smoother, remove the skins of the chickpeas beforehand. I usually leave them on to increase the fiber in the recipes.

Next, mince the olives and the parsley.

Consecutively, transfer the hummus in a large bowl and combine it with the remaining compounds – olives, parsley, the spices, chickpea flour, baking powder, pectin, the tahini, and salt.

Stir and blend the ingredients as much as possible.

If the mixture is too dry and hard to blend, add a little bit of water to make the process easier.

Now start heating the oven to 200° C/ 392° F.

Next, transfer the mixture in a bread baking mold covered with parchment paper.

Sprinkle the sunflower seeds on top and bake for about an hour.

My notes:

Chickpea Bread

Ingredients:

8 Tbsps. **Chickpea flour**
4 Tbsps. **Flax seed flour**
1 Tbsp. **Ground flax seeds**
Salt, cumin, ground coriander seeds – to taste
4 Tbsps. **Olive oil**
2 **Eggs**
1 tsp. **Baking powder**
4 Tbsps. **Seeds** (poppy, sunflower, sesame, pumpkin, etc.)

Instructions:

Mix the chickpea flour, the flax seed flour and the ground flax seeds with some water to form a mixture with a semi-liquid thick consistency.

Add the spices and leave the batter to rest for about 8 hours or overnight for the flours to absorb some of the liquid.

Next, beat the eggs and add them to the mixture along with the remaining ingredients.

Heat the oven to 180° C/ 356° F.

Pour the bread mixture in a baking mold (with approx. 6"-7" diameter) and bake until fully cooked.

Check with a toothpick to see if the bread is ready. It may take a while for all the water to evaporate.

Enjoy!

Protein Bread I

Ingredients:

4 **Eggs**
1 cup **Boiled chickpeas** (or canned)
1 tsp. **Baking powder**
2 Tbsps. **Sunflower seeds**
2 tsps. **Poppy seeds**
2 tsps. **Flax seeds**
2 tsps. **Sesame seeds**

Instructions:

Place the eggs, the chickpeas, and the baking powder in a blender and homogenize the mixture.

Next, simply add the seeds and stir nicely.

Now you can start heating the oven to 180° C/ 356° F.

Pour the batter in a bread mold and bake for about 20 minutes.

Wait for the pastry to cool down before cutting it.

You can store this bread in the fridge for up to 3 days.

My notes:

Protein Bread II

Ingredients:

1 cup **Cottage cheese**
5 **Eggs**
3 1/2 Tbsps. **Buckwheat flour**
1/2 cup **Ground almonds**
1/2 cup **Ground flax seeds**
2 tsps. **Baking powder**
1 tsp. **Salt**

Instructions:

Start by heating the oven to 170° C/ 338° F.

Now blend the dry ingredients in a bowl – the buckwheat flour, ground almonds, flax seeds, baking powder, and the salt.

Next, add the cottage cheese and the eggs.

Stir and blend the mixture until you have nice soft dough.

Transfer to a bread baking mold and cook for about an hour.

Remember to check with a toothpick to see if the bread is ready. If not, leave it to bake for several more minutes until fully cooked.

When the toothpick comes out clean, take the bread out of the oven and leave it cool down a bit for about 10 minutes.

After that, you can remove it from its mold and leave it aside to reduce its temperature completely.

Note that this bread can be a bit moist on the inside, so store it in the fridge for up to 2-3 days.

Cabbage Bread

Ingredients:

For the dough:
2 cups **Gluten-free flour mix of choice**
1 tsp. **Dry yeast**
1 tsp. **Salt**
2-3 Tbsps. **Olive oil**
1 cup **Lukewarm water**

For the filling:
1/4 average **Cabbage**
Salt – to taste
1 **Egg**
3-4 Tbsps. **Sour cream**
1/2 cup **Feta cheese**
Some spices of choice (paprika, pepper, fennel) – to taste

Instructions:

First, we start preparing the dough.

Simply blend all ingredients until you have soft non-sticky dough. Add more flour, if you need to reach that consistency.

Knead the mixture for several minutes, cover it with a kitchen towel, and leave it aside to rest and rise.

Meanwhile, we can make the filling.

Mince the cabbage in small pieces and mix it with some salt.

Add the sour cream and the spices and blend again nicely.

Now we can start assembling the bread.

Take a sheet of baking paper and place it on the kitchen counter (or table).

Roll out the dough on top in the form of a rectangle (as much as you can).

Place the filling at the center of the bread sheet leaving some space at both ends. Now wrap the filling with the extra dough we left from the previous step to fully cover the cabbage mixture.

Next, heat the oven to 200° C/ 392° F and transfer the bread with the parchment paper in a baking pan.

Bake until the dish is fully cooked and golden.

You can also grease the pastry with some butter before placing it in the oven for extra deliciousness!

My notes:

Tasty Bread with Seeds and Veggies

Ingredients:

2 **Eggs**
1 cup **Yogurt**
1/2 tsp. **Baking soda**
1 tsp. **Sea salt**
1 tsp. **Garlic powder**
2 Tbsps. **Olive oil**
4 Tbsps. (heaped) **Ground flax seeds**
1/2 cup **Pumpkin seed flour**
1/2 cup **Sesame flour**
1 cup **Chickpea flour**
1 cup **Lukewarm water**
1/2 cup **Olives** (sliced)
1 **Red pepper**
1 **Green pepper**
Some **Butter**

Instructions:

First, we can start by heating the oven to 180° C/ 356° F.

Next, mix the yogurt with the baking soda and wait for it to start frothing.

Consecutively, take a large bowl and mix the bubbly yogurt with the eggs, salt, garlic powder, olive oil, flax seeds, the gluten-free flours, and the water.

Blend the mixture well with a hand mixer or a blender.

The batter will be a bit thinner, because the flax seeds will absorb most of the liquid.

Next, dice the peppers and slice the olives, if not done so already.

Add them to the bread mixture and stir with a fork to spread them evenly.

Take a baking pan and grease it with the butter.

Pour the mixture in and bake until fully cooked!

Bon Appetite!

Pea Bread with Stinging Nettle

Ingredients:

Dry ingredients:
1 Tbsp. **Baking soda**
1/2 tsp. **Muscovado sugar** (or coconut sugar)
1/2 tsp. **Himalayan salt**
1 1/2 cup **Pea flour**
3 1/2 Tbsps. **Rice flour**
3 1/2 Tbsps. **Flax seed powder**
1 Tbsp. **Stinging nettle powder**
1 Tbsp. **Savory**
1 Tbsp. **Fenugreek**
1/2 tsp. **Coriander**

Liquid ingredients:
1 1/2 Tbsp. **Lemon juice** (or apple cider vinegar)
1 1/2 cup **Warm water**

Some **Butter**

Instructions:

First, mix all the dry ingredients in a large bowl and blend them well.

In another container, combine the liquid compounds – the lemon juice and the water.

Make a hole in the center of the dry mix – just like the crater we usually make for preparing bread dough.

Next, slowly start pouring the liquid inside this cavity while mixing and blending.

The result should be soft bread dough.

Now you can start heating the oven to 180° C/ 356° F.

Take a suitable baking mold and grease it nicely with the butter. Make sure you cover all of the insides of the container. Sprinkle some gluten-free flour on top to prevent from the bread to stick to the mold.

Alternatively, you can use baking paper as well.

Transfer the bread mixture inside and spread more butter on top of it.

Bake in the pre-heated oven for about 40 minutes (until fully cooked).

Finally, when the bread is ready, leave it in the container for not longer than 10 minutes to rest.

Next, take it out and let it cool down for 10-15 more minutes on a grid.

Store the bread wrapped in a clean kitchen towel.

Fast and Easy Pita Bread

Ingredients:

1/2 cup **Buckwheat flour**
1 cup **Yogurt**
1 **Egg**
1 tsp. **Olive oil**
1 tsp. **Apple cider vinegar** (or balsamic vinegar)
1/2 tsp. **Baking soda**
A pinch of **Salt**

Instructions:

First, mix the baking soda with the vinegar.

Next, place the flour in a bowl, add the remaining ingredients and stir with a fork for not longer than 1 minute.

Now take a flat baking pan and cover it with parchment paper.

Pour the mixture and spread it gently with the fork (the thickness will be about 1 cm and approx. half an inch).

The pita will be very thin, but extremely tasty!

Next, heat the oven to 150° C/ 302° F. If your oven has a fan, you can switch it on.

Bake the pita for about 20 minutes in the well pre-heated oven.

Bread with Cream Cheese

Ingredients:

4 **Eggs**
1 1/2 cup **Yogurt**
1 Tbsp. **Baking soda**
1 Tbsp. **Salt**
1/2 Tbsp. **White pepper**
2 Tbsps. **Caraway**
1/3 cup **Olive oil**
1 cup **Rice flour**
1/2 cup **Chickpea flour**
1/2 cup **Corn flour**
1/2 cup **Tapioca flour**
1/2 cup **Cream cheese**

Instructions:

First, beat the eggs in a large bowl.

Next, mix the yogurt with the baking soda and let it froth for a bit.

Consecutively, mix the bubbly yogurt with the eggs and blend them well.

Start adding the remaining ingredients one by one as you continue to stir and homogenize the mixture.

Now heat the oven to 180° C/ 356° F.

Take a large cake baking mold and grease it with some olive oil.

Transfer the mixture into the container and bake for about 30 minutes until fully cooked.

Easy Bread (for Home Bread Machine) I

Ingredients:

2 cups **Gluten-free flour mix of choice**
2 **Eggs**
1 Tbsp. **Apple cider vinegar**
2 tsps. **Vegan gluten-free baking yeast powder**
2 Tbsps. **Butter** (soft)
1 1/2 cup **Water**
2 tsps. **Salt**
1 1/2 Tbsp. **Muscovado sugar** (or coconut sugar)

Instructions:

This recipe is very easy to prepare because we basically let the appliance do the job for us.

It is best to have a home bread making machine with a special gluten-free program. The process of kneading, rising the dough, and baking a loaf of gluten-free bread is a bit different from the regular wheat products.

So, simply place the ingredients in the bread maker and switch on the appropriate program.

My notes:

Easy Bread (for Home Bread Machine) II

Ingredients:

1 1/2 cup **Warm water**
1 tsp. **Salt**
2 1/2 Tbsps. **Quinoa flour** (or ground quinoa seeds)
1 1/2 Tbsp. **Rice flour**
1 1/2 cup **Gluten-free flour mix**
1/2 tsp. **Dry yeast**
5 Tbsps. **Seeds** (sesame, sunflower, poppy, chia, etc.)

Instructions:

Start adding the ingredients in your bread machine one by one in the order they are listed.

Switch the appliance on the gluten-free program and let it do its job.

Then, when the bread is ready, take it out, wrap it in a kitchen towel, and leave it to cool down completely for about 2 hours.

After that, you can cut and consume!
Enjoy!

My notes:

Brazilian Bread Buns

Ingredients:

2 cups **Tapioca starch**
1/2 cup **Water**
1/2 cup **Coconut milk**
4 **Eggs**
Salt – to taste
1 cup **Sunflower oil**
1 cup **Grated yellow cheese**

Instructions:

Place the tapioca starch in a large bowl.

Next, mix the coconut milk, the water, and the salt in a metal pot and heat them.

When the liquid starts to boil, take it off the heat.

Next, slowly and gently start pouring the mixture in the bowl with the tapioca. Remember to stir the entire time to prevent from any lumps to form.

The goal is to have non-sticky dough mixture, so add more tapioca, if needed.

Next, add the eggs, the oil, and the grated cheese, and continue to knead and blend the dough.

Take a suitable flat baking pan and cover it with parchment paper.

Scoop from the dough and form small balls which will be our delicious Brazilian bread buns.

You can grease your hands with some oil to make the molding easier.

Arrange the balls in the pan, but remember to leave room between them because they will rise during the thermal treatment.

Bake for about half an hour and leave these goodies to cool down completely.

Beware! They are extremely addictive!

Vegetable Bread Buns

Ingredients:

2 1/2 cups **Rice flour**
2 **Eggs**
1 tsp. **Baking soda**
1/4 cup **Yogurt**
Some **Water**
Vegetables of choice – spinach, broccoli, parsley, mushrooms, etc.
Some **Cheese**
Salt and spices – to taste

Instructions:

This recipe is very easy and it could be tweaked and changed according to your preferences and desires.

The quantities of the veggies and the types of spices you use are totally up to you! Feel free to experiment and let your imagination run wild!

Here is how it's done!

First, mix the baking soda with the yogurt and let it froth for a bit.

Next, beat the eggs in a large bowl, and add the flour, the bubbly yogurt, and the spices.

Blend the mixture well, and leave it aside for a bit.

Next, dice the vegetables and the cheese in small cubes and add them to the mixture.

If the batter is too dry and difficult to mold, add some water until you reach the necessary non-sticky consistency.

Now you can start heating the oven to 180° C/ 356° F.

Start forming the buns as medium balls and arrange them in a baking tray covered with parchment paper.

Bake the snacks for about 20 minutes and enjoy!

Fast & Easy Bread Bites (Low Carb)

Ingredients:

2 **Eggs**
3 Tbsps. **Sesame seeds**
1 Tbsp. **Coconut flour**
Salt - to taste

Instructions:

Start by heating the oven to 175° C/ 347° F. Use the fan, if you have it.

Next, beat the eggs in a bowl and blend them with the salt and the sesame seeds.

Now add the coconut flour and stir again. Leave the mixture for a bit to bulk up and rise.

Next, take a small baking pan and cover it with parchment paper.

Pour the batter in and bake for about 15 minutes.

Let the bread cool down and cut it in the desired shapes and sizes.

Zucchini Bread Bites (Low Carb)

Ingredients:

1 small **Zucchini**
6 Tbsps. **Almond flour**
2 **Eggs**
1 Tbsp. **Seed mix** (sesame, pumpkin, flax)
1 Tbsp. **Coconut butter**
Salt and Oregano – to taste
1/2 tsp. **Garlic powder**

Instructions:

First, grate the zucchini (or mince it in a kitchen chopper) and squeeze out its juice as much as possible.

In another bowl, beat the eggs and blend them with the remaining ingredients.

Finally, add the zucchini puree and blend again until fully homogeneous.

Now heat the oven to 180° C/ 356° F and switch on the fan, if you have it.

Take a flat baking pan and cover it with parchment paper.

Grease it for extra protection and pour the batter in.

Press gently to form a thin layer and bake for about 20 minutes.

Switch off the oven and leave the dish for a couple more minutes until golden.

Let the bread cool off completely before cutting it in the desired shapes.

Gluten-free Buns

Ingredients:

1 1/2 tsp. **Yeast** (gluten-free)
1 cup **Warm water**
2 tsps. **Maple syrup**
Some **Rice flour**
2 **Eggs**
2 Tbsps. **Yogurt**
Salt – to taste
4 Tbsps. **Potato starch**
3 1/2 Tbsps. **Butter** (melted)
Some **Grated cheese** (white or yellow)

Instructions:

First, mix the yeast with the warm water, the maple syrup and 2 Tbsps. of the rice flour. Stir well and leave the mixture to bulge up.

In the meantime, beat the eggs in a bowl and blend them with the yogurt and the salt.

Next, add the yeast and blend again.

Consecutively, add the potato starch and some rice flour.

Knead the mixture until you have soft and pliable dough. Add as much rice flour as you need to reach that consistency.

Next, add the melted butter and continue to knead and blend the dough.

It should be soft and a little bit sticky.

Now you can start heating the oven to 180° C/ 356° F.

Meanwhile, commence making the buns themselves.

Scoop some of the dough, press it gently and put some of the cheese in the middle. Roll the bun so that the dairy product remains inside the pastry.

Place it in a baking tray with parchment paper and repeat the process with the remaining dough.

Bake in the pre-heated oven until fully cooked!

My notes:

Spinach Buns

Ingredients:

For the buns:
2 cups **Cassava flour**
2 Tbsps. **Coconut flour**
1/3 cup **Arrowroot starch**
A pinch of **Salt**
2 **Eggs**
1/4 cup **Olive oil**
2/3 cup **Warm water**
3-4 tsps. **Dry yeast**
2 Tbsps. **Honey**

For the filling:
2 cups **Spinach**
1 cup **Wild garlic**

Instructions:

First, mix the yeast with the warm water and the honey. Stir to dissolve the bee product and leave the mixture aside to start frothing and rising.

Next, beat the eggs and add them to the yeast along with the olive oil.

Now mix the dry ingredients (cassava flour, coconut flour, arrowroot starch, salt) in a large bowl and blend them well.

Next, gently start pouring the liquid mixture in thin stream while stirring and blending the compounds.

The goal is to have soft and non-sticky dough. If you need to, add more starch to reach that consistency.

Next, cover the bowl with some kitchen foil and leave the dough to rise in a warm room for about an hour.

After that, knead for several minutes.

Now divide the mixture into 4 equal parts and roll them out in thin squares.

Next, we will prepare the filling.

Cut the leafy greens in medium pieces and let them soften in a hot pan with a little bit of water.

Separate the green mixture into 4 parts for each bun.

Wrap the filling with the pastry layers and we are ready for the final part.

Heat the oven to 200° C/ 392° and bake for about 25-30 minutes until golden.

Bon appetite!

My notes:

Gluten-free Fiber Hamburger Buns

Ingredients:

3 Tbsps. **Almond flour**
1 Tbsp. **Rice flour**
4 Tbsps. **Psyllium Husk**
Salt – to taste
1/2 cup **Hot water**
1 tsp. **Baking soda**
2 Tbsps. **Apple cider vinegar** (ACV)
4 **Egg whites**

Instructions:

Mix the baking soda with the ACV and wait for the chemical reaction to subside.

Next, simply add all the remaining ingredients and blend well.

At this point, you can switch on the oven at 160° C/ 320° F.

Now we can start forming the buns.

Take a baking tray and cover it with parchment paper.

Scoop some of the dough, form it as a small ball and press it gently to make it flat. Place it on the baking tray and repeat for the rest of the buns.

Bake for about 25 minutes until golden. Then, you can switch off the oven, open the door, and leave the buns inside until the furnace cools down.

Quick Hamburger Bun in a Cup

microwave

Ingredients:

1 Tbsp. **Butter** (melted)
1 **Egg**
1 Tbsp. **Coconut flour**
1 Tbsp. **Apple flour**
1 tsp. **Lemon juice** (or apple cider vinegar)
A pinch of **Baking soda**
A pinch of **Salt**
A pinch of **Ginger powder**

Instructions:

Take a small ceramic cup (microwave safe) and grease it with the melted butter.

Next, beat the egg inside the cup.

Start adding all the remaining ingredients one by one (as they are listed) while continuously stirring and blending the mixture.

Remember to scrape the sides of the cup and homogenize the batter to remove any lumps.

Place the cup in the microwave oven and cook for about 1-2 minutes at maximum power.

If you do not wish to use the microwave, simply bake the bun in the oven at 200° C/ 392° F for 15 minutes (until fully cooked).

Cut the bun in two and stuff with your favorite ingredients!

Guilt-free Hamburger Buns (Low Carb)

Ingredients:

3 **Eggs**
A pinch of **Salt**
1/2 tsp. **Baking soda**
3-4 Tbsps. **Buffalo yogurt** (or cream cheese, sour cream)

Instructions:

First, separate the egg yolks from the whites.

Next, beat the egg whites until stiff along with the salt and the baking powder.

After that, beat the egg yolks and blend them with the yogurt.

Next, gently combine both mixtures and stir with a spatula to preserve the volume of the egg whites as much as possible.

At this point, you can start heating the oven to 150° C/ 302° F.

Take a baking tray and cover it with parchment paper.

Finally, scoop from the batter and place it on the baking pan.

Bake the buns for about 20-30 minutes (depending on your oven) until golden.

Remember – the pastries will rise and bulge up a lot in the oven, but they will quickly lose their volume once you take them off the heat. This is completely normal, so don't worry about it!

Bon appetite!

2-Ingredient Potato Pancakes (Vegan)

Ingredients:

3 large **Potatoes**
1 cup **Gluten-free flour mix**

Instructions:

First, boil the potatoes and mash them (or grate them).
Then simply add the flour and blend completely.

The ratio between the potato puree and the flour should be about 3:1. So, if the boiled rhizomes are about 2 1/2 cups, the amount of flour should be a little less than a cup.

The goal is to have hard homogeneous dough.

Divide it into several parts and roll out each one into thin pancakes. Frequently sprinkle some flour to make the process easier because the dough might be a bit sticky.

Next, heat a non-stick pan without adding any oil or butter and bake the pancakes on each side until fully cooked.

Garnish with whatever you prefer.

My notes:

Green Pancakes

Ingredients:

2 cups **Baby spinach**
2 **Eggs**
1/2 tsp. **Baking soda**
A pinch of **Tartaric acid**
1 Tbsp. **Water**
2-3 Tbsps. **Coconut butter**
Some **Almond flour**

Instructions:

Mince and puree the spinach in a kitchen chopper or a robot.

Next, beat the eggs and mix them with the leafy greens.

Combine the baking soda with the tartaric acid and the water.

Transfer the mixture to the spinach and eggs.

Add the coconut butter and almond flour until you have the consistency of pancake batter.

Bake the crepes in a hot non-stick pan on both sides as usual.

Garnish with whatever you prefer!

GLUTEN-FREE PIZZA

Low Crab Gluten-free Pizza Crust (with Extra Fiber)

Ingredients:

4 **Eggs**
2 Tbsps. (heaped) **Yogurt**
3 1/2 Tbsps. **Coconut flour**
2 tsps. **Psyllium Husk**
1 tsp. **Salt**
1 tsp. **Baking powder**

Instructions:

First, beat the eggs in a large bowl.

Next, add all the remaining ingredients while stirring with a fork.

Blend the mixture well to remove any lumps and homogenize it fully.

You should reach the consistency of soft pizza dough that is very pliable and easy to mold.

Spread the crust in a baking tray covered with parchment paper.

Now you can garnish the pizza with whatever you desire – tomato puree, sausages, cheese, veggies, mushrooms, etc.

Heat the oven to the usual 180° C/ 356° F and bake the pizza for about 15-20 minutes until it is fully cooked and nicely crunchy.

Vegan Gluten-free Pizza Crust

Ingredients:

1/2 cup **Chickpea flour**
3-4 Tbsps. **Sorghum flour**
1/2 cup **Buckwheat flour**
1 tsp. **Salt**
1/2 tsp. **Baking soda**
1/2 tsp. **Muscovado sugar** (or organic brown sugar)
1/2 tsp. **Baking powder**
1/2 tsp. **Apple cider vinegar** (ACV)
1/2 cup **Lukewarm water**

Instructions:

The preparation of this recipe is very simple.

Blend the ingredients completely until the mixture is fully homogenous.

If you need to, adjust the quantities of the flour and/or the water to reach the desired consistency of thick dough.

Spread the pizza crust in a baking tray covered with parchment paper.

Garnish with your favorite toppings and bake in a preheated oven (180° C/ 356° F) until fully cooked and nicely crunchy!

Corn Pizza Crust

Ingredients:

1 **Egg**
1/2 cup **Yogurt**
A pinch of **Baking soda**
A pinch of **Salt**
Corn flour (non-GMO)
Some **Butter** (or olive oil, coconut butter, etc.)

Instructions:

Mix the yogurt with the baking soda and leave it to froth for a bit.

Next, beat the egg and blend it with the bubbly yogurt and the salt.

Start adding the flour until you have nice soft and pliable non-stocky dough.

Take a baking pan and cover it with parchment paper.

Grease it with some butter for extra protection, and spread the dough in the pan.

Now heat the oven to 180° C/ 356° F.

Bake the crust until half-cooked and take it out of the furnace.

Garnish your pizza with whatever ingredients you prefer and bring the dish back in the oven.

Switch to 200° C/ 392° F and bake until fully cooked.

Mini Pizza Crusts (Vegan)

Ingredients:

5-6 **Button mushrooms**
1/2 cup **Frozen peas**
6 Tbsps. (heaped) **Corn flour**
2 pinches of **Salt**
Spices (pepper, cumin, oregano, savory) – to taste
1 cup **Water**

Instructions:

First, mince the buttons in small pieces (use a kitchen chopper for ease).

Next, grind the peas as well and mix them with the mushrooms.

Add the flour, the salt, and the other spices, and blend completely.

Start heating the oven to 180° C/ 356° F.

Now slowly add the water to the mixture as you continuously stir and blend the pizza dough.

Add as much liquid as to reach a thick consistency – not like a typical dough, and not too liquid either.

Take a baking tray and cover it parchment paper.

Scoop from the batter and form the pizza crusts.

Bake until golden, then flip them to bake on the other side.

When the pizzas are almost ready, garnish them with your favorite topping and bake for 10-15 more minutes.

Perfect afternoon snacks!

Red Lentil Pizza Crust (Vegan)

Ingredients:

3/4 cup **Red lentils**
3/4 cup **Water**
1 tsp. **Olive oil**
1/2 tsp. **Salt**
1 tsp. **Baking powder**

Instructions:

First, soak the lentils in some clean water for about 12 hours.

Then, strain the legumes and wash them thoroughly.

Consecutively, blend them with 3/4 cup water in a blender or a kitchen chopper.

Add the remaining ingredients and blend completely.

Switch on the oven at 180° C/ 356° F. You can use the fan, if you have it.

While you wait for the oven, take a baking tray and cover it parchment paper.

Pour the pizza "dough" and bake for 30 minutes. Then, you can garnish the crust with whatever you desire, and continue cooking the pizza for about 20 more minutes.

Quinoa Pizza Crust

Ingredients:

3/4 cup **Quinoa**
1 tsp. **Baking powder**
1/2 - 1 tsp. **Salt**
1 **Egg**
2-3 Tbsps. **Olive oil**
Spices (rosemary, garlic powder, oregano) – to taste

Instructions:

We need to start preparing this recipe from the previous day.

Soak the quinoa in some clean water overnight and wash it thoroughly the next day.

Strain it from the water and remove any excess liquid as much as possible.

Next, mince the grains (actually pseudo-grains ☺) in a kitchen chopper until you reach a mustard resembling consistency.

Now simply add the remaining ingredients and blend again.

Pour the batter in a baking pan covered with parchment paper.

Gently spread the mixture to form a crust with about 3 mm/ 0,1 inch width (something like a crepe).

Heat the oven to 180° C/ 356° F and bake the dish until golden.

Then, flip it and garnish with whatever you desire.

Finally, leave the pizza to bake until fully cooked.

Eggplant Pizzas (Low Carb)

This recipe is fairly easy to prepare and the quantities can be tweaked and adjusted to your preferences and needs.

Ingredients:

1 **Eggplant**
1 cup **Tomato sauce**
3-4 cloves **Garlic**
1/2 cup **Cheese** (mozzarella, cheddar, etc.)
Some **Olive oil**
Some **Parmesan**
Fresh Basil leaves

Instructions:

First, cut the eggplant in slices with approximately 1 cm/0.4 inch width.

Arrange the slices in a baking pan covered with parchment paper.

Sprinkle some olive oil on top and roast the veggies in a hot oven (200° C/ 392° F) on both sides until golden.

Now mix the tomato puree with the garlic cloves and blend them in a chopper or a blender.

Slice the cheese, cut the cherry tomatoes in halves, and grate the parmesan.

Now we can arrange the pizzas.

Spread the tomato sauce on top of the eggplants, add some cheese slices, the cherry tomatoes, and the parmesan.

Bring the dish back in the oven for about 10 more minutes until the cheese is fully melted.

Serve with fresh basil leaves.

Zucchini Pizza (Low Carb)

Ingredients:

For the crust:
1 **Zucchini**
1 **Egg**
4 Tbsps. **Almond flour**
1/2 cup **Cheese**
Some **Garlic powder and oregano** – to taste

For the topping:
Tomato puree
1/2 cup **Bacon**
1 **Bell pepper**
1 cup **Mozzarella**
Some **Parmesan or cheddar**

Instructions:

First, grate (or mince) the zucchini, sprinkle some salt, and place it in a colander.

Leave it aside to secret its juice for about half an hour.

Next, squeeze any liquid left and place the veggie in a bowl.

Add the almond flour and the egg.

Grate the cheese and add it to the mix.

Add the spices and blend well.

Transfer the mixture to a baking pan covered with parchment paper.

Spread nicely with a fork to make an even crust.

Heat the oven to 180° C/ 356° F and switch on the fan.

Bake the pizza crust for about 15 minutes.

Meanwhile, dice the bacon, grate the parmesan, slice the mozzarella and the pepper.

Finally, garnish the dish with the topping and bake for 10 more minutes.

That's it!

Omelette Pizza

Ingredients:

For the crust:
1 cup **Quinoa**
1 **Egg**
1 tsp. **Salt**
1 tsp. **Baking powder**
3-4 Tbsps. **Olive oil**
A little bit of **Water**

For the omelette:
3 **Eggs**
Feta cheese – to taste
Yellow cheese – to taste

Instructions:

Soak the quinoa grains in some water overnight (about 12 hours).

Strain them the next day and wash them thoroughly with clean water.

Place the quinoa and all the remaining ingredients for the pizza crust in a blender or a kitchen chopper and homogenize the mixture.

Add as much water as to make it easier for the appliance to puree the compounds.

Heat the oven to 200° C/ 392° F.

Spread the quinoa mixture on a baking pan covered with parchment paper and bake for several minutes (approx. 7).

Meanwhile, grate the cheese and mash the feta cheese.

Mix them with the eggs and whisk to homogenize the mixture.

Pour the omelette on top of the quinoa crust and bake until fully cooked.

Voila!

My notes:

GLUTEN-FREE PASTRIES FROM THE BALKANS

Gluten-free Pita I

Ingredients:

1 cup **Rice flour**
1 **Egg**
1 cup **Yogurt**
1/2 tsp. **Baking soda**
1 Tbsp. **Olive oil**
Savory – to taste
Salt – to taste
Some **Seeds** of choice – sunflower, pumpkin, poppy, etc.

Instructions:

Heat the oven to 180° C/ 356° F.

Mix the yogurt with the baking soda and wait for it to start forming bubbles.

Next, simply blend all ingredients (except the seeds) completely with a hand mixer or a blender.

After that, take a baking pan and cover it with parchment paper.

Pour the mixture in and sprinkle the seeds on top for decoration.

Bake the pita until fully cooked and until golden.

Gluten-free Pita II

Ingredients:

2 cups **Gluten-free flour mix of choice**
1 1/2 cup **Lukewarm water**
2 **Eggs**
2 tsps. **Dry yeast**
1/2 tsp. **Muscovado sugar** (or organic brown sugar)
1/2 cup **Butter**
3 Tbsps. **Olive oil**
1 1/2 cup **Feta cheese**
1 tsp. (heaped) **Salt**

Instructions:

First, we need to prepare the yeast.

Mix it with the water and the brown sugar, and leave it to rise for several minutes.

Next, add the flour, the eggs, olive oil, the salt, and the mashed feta cheese. Stir and blend the ingredients completely until the mixture becomes fully homogeneous.

Alternatively, if you wish to leave the feta cheese in small chunks in the pita, just add it after you have blended the dough.

Consecutively, melt the butter on low temperature.

Take out your favorite bread baking mold and grease it thoroughly with some of the melted butter.

Next, pour the remaining of the butter in the pita dough and blend again.

Place the mixture in the baking mold and switch on the oven to 60° C / 140° F and leave the pita inside to rise for about 20 minutes.

Finally, change the temperature to 180° C/ 356° F and bake until fully cooked!

Gluten-free Burek (Banitsa) I

Ingredients:

1 cup **Buckwheat flakes**
3 **Eggs**
1 cup **Feta cheese** (mashed)
1 cup **Yogurt**
3 1/2 Tbsps. **Milk**
1 tsp. **Baking powder**
3 1/2 Tbsps. **Butter**

Instructions:

First, start heating the oven to 200° C/ 392° F.

Next, we can prepare the burek itself which takes very little time!

Mix all the ingredients in a large bowl and blend them with a hand mixer or a blender.

Take a baking pan and cover it with parchment paper. Moist the paper a little bit and pour the mixture in the pan.

Bake in the pre-heated oven until fully cooked and golden.

Gluten-free Burek (Banitsa) II

Ingredients:

1 cup **Buckwheat flakes**
4 **Eggs**
1 cup **Goat cheese** (mashed)
1 1/2 cup **Goat yogurt**
2-3 Tbsps. **Coconut butter** (melted)
1 tsp. **Baking soda**
1-2 Tbsps. **Apple cider vinegar** (ACV)
Salt – to taste

Instructions:

First, beat the eggs in a large bowl.

Mash the goat cheese and add it to the eggs.

Next, add some salt, the baking soda, and the buckwheat flakes, and blend completely.

Consecutively, add the yogurt and the ACV.

Blend again and add the coconut butter.

Stir and homogenize the batter and it is ready for the final part.

Heat the oven to 180° C/ 356° F, and bake the banitsa for about 45 minutes (until fully cooked and when the toothpick comes out clean).

Easy Gluten-free Spanakopita

Ingredients:

24 **Rice spring rolls wrappers** (with approx. 8-9 inch diameter)
3 **Eggs**
1 cup **Yogurt**
A pinch of **Baking soda**
1 cup **Baby spinach**
1 cup **Goat cheese**
4-5 Tbsps. **Ghee butter**
1-2 Tbsps. **Cow butter**

Instructions:

First, we are going to prepare the spinach filling.

Soak the leafy greens in some clean water for about 30 minutes.

Next, strain and wash them thoroughly.

Mince the spinach in small pieces and place it in a hot skillet with some cow butter.

Stir on low temperature until the greens become fully soft.

Consecutively, mix the yogurt with the baking soda and let it froth for a bit.

Beat the eggs in a bowl and blend them with the bubbly yogurt and the cooked spinach.

At this point, you can switch on the oven at 180° C/ 356° F. You can switch on the fan, if you have it.

Now we can start assembling the spanakopita and we are going to need a cup or a bowl of warm water.

Take a baking pan and cover it with parchment paper.

Next, take a spring roll wrapper and soak it in the warm water for about 20 seconds until it softens.

Place it in the baking pan and cover with the spinach filling. Sprinkle some mashed goat cheese and pour a little bit of melted ghee.

Repeat the process until you are out of rice sheets.

If the wrappers are too thin, you can place two or three of them for each layer.

Cover the last sheet with melted ghee and the pastry is ready for the final part.

Bake the spanakopita in the heated oven until fully cooked and golden.

Lazy Spanakopita with Feta Cheese

Ingredients:

1 cup **Spinach leaves**
3-4 Tbsps. **Olive oil** (or butter)
5 **Eggs**
1 cup **Yogurt**
1 tsp. **Baking soda**
1 cup **Rice flour**
1/2 cup **Chickpea flour**
1 tsp. **Salt**
1/2 cup **Feta cheese** (adjust to taste)

Instructions:

Wash the spinach and cut it in medium stripes.

Heat the olive oil in a saucepan and add the leafy greens.

Pour just a little bit of water and put the lid on. Cook the spinach until it softens.

Meanwhile, mix the yogurt with the baking soda and let it froth for a minute or two.

Next, beat the eggs in a large bowl and blend them with the bubbly yogurt, the two types of flour, and the salt.

When the spinach is ready and fully cooled down, add it to the main mixture along with the mashed feta cheese. Stir with a fork to blend the ingredients well.

Heat the oven to 200° C/ 392° F and bake the pastry for about 30 minutes until fully cooked.

Enjoy!

My notes:

Lazy Winter Burek with Leek

Ingredients:

1 cup **Gluten-free flour mix**
1/2 cup **Chickpea flour**
5 **Eggs**
1 cup **Kefir**
1 tsp. **Baking soda**
1-2 cups **Leek**
1-2 Tbsps. **Cow butter**

Instructions:

First, mince the leek in medium pieces and place it in a skillet or a saucepan.

Add the cow butter and stir on low heat until soft.

Take it off the heat and leave it to cool down.

Next, mix the kefir with the baking soda and wait a bit for it to froth.

After that, beat the eggs in a bowl and blend them with the bubbly dairy product, and the two types of flour.

Finally, add the soft leek and stir again.

Now heat the oven to 200° C/ 392° F and bake the burek until fully cooked!

Rice Banitsa Rolls

Ingredients:

12-13 **Rice sheets** (approx. 8" in diameter)
3 **Eggs**
1 cup **Feta cheese** (mashed)
1 tsp. **Fenugreek**
Some **Butter**

Instructions:

First, beat the eggs and mash the feta cheese.
Mix them both and add the fenugreek powder.
Heat some clean water and dip each rice sheet in it for a few seconds to soften.

Put the moist rice sheet in a plate and place 1-2 tablespoons of the mixture on top.

Next, fold the sheet just like you would do with a spring roll.

Repeat this process until you finish with all the rice sheets.

At this point, you can start heating the oven to 180° C/ 356° F.

Next, take a baking pan (with about 9" diameter), cover it with parchment paper, and arrange all the rolls inside. Place them as tight as possible.

Spread some butter on top and put the banitsa in the oven.

Bake the burek for about 20-25 minutes until fully cooked. You can switch on the fan, if you have it.

Check to see if the meal is ready with a wooden toothpick.

Enjoy!

Leek and Mushroom Banitsa Rolls

Ingredients:

14-16 **Rice sheets** (approx. 8" in diameter)
4 large **Leeks**
1 cup **Button mushrooms**
2-3 Tbsps. **Unscented coconut butter** (or regular cow butter)
2 **Eggs**
5-6 Tbsps. **Soda** (carbonated water)
Salt, paprika, pepper – to taste

Instructions:

First, mince the leeks and mushrooms in small pieces or grind them in a kitchen chopper (separately).

Next, heat the butter in a large saucepan and place the green vegetable inside.

Put the lid on and let the leeks stew until they soften.

Next, add the mushrooms, the spices, and let the mixture cook for several more minutes (until the mushrooms soften a bit as well).

Now take a small baking pan (about 8 inches in diameter) and cover it with parchment paper.

Also, prepare a cup with warm water for the rice sheets.

Next, grease the pan with some of the butter and we are ready to assemble the banitsa.

Soak one rice sheet in the water for about 20 seconds and place it in the pan. Sprinkle several drops melted butter and add one more layer.

Next, spread some of the leek and mushroom filling and repeat the process with all the remaining layers.

The final tier should be two rice sheets at the top.

Next, heat the oven at 180° C/ 356° F and switch on the fan, if you have it.

Meanwhile, beat the eggs and mix them with the soda.

Pour the mixture on top of the dish and it is ready for the final part!

Bake for about 20-30 minutes until fully cooked.

My notes:

Rice Balkan Burek (Tutmanik)

Ingredients:

2 **Eggs**
1/2 tsp. **Salt**
1/2 tsp. **Garlic powder**
1 cup **Yogurt**
1/2 tsp. **Baking soda**
2 Tbsps. **Butter** (melted)
1 – 1 1/2 cup **Rice flour**
1/2 cup **Cream cheese spread**
1/2 cup **Feta cheese** (mashed)
Some seeds of choice – **poppy, sunflower, pumpkin**, etc. – for decoration

Instructions:

First, heat the oven to the usual 180° C/ 356° F.

Next, mix the yogurt with the baking soda and wait for it to start frothing.

Consecutively, blend all ingredients (except the feta cheese) in a large bowl.

Next, add the mashed feta, stir gently with a fork, and our burek mixture is ready!

Sprinkle the seeds on top and place in the oven.

Bake the dish until fully cooked (about 30 minutes) – the toothpick should come out clean.

Tutmanik with Yellow Cheese

Ingredients:

1 cup **Yellow cheese**
1 1/2 cup **Yogurt**
A pinch of **Salt**
2 tsps. **Baking powder**
3 **Eggs**
1 Tbsp. **Savory**
Buckwheat flour
Some seeds of choice – **poppy, sunflower, pumpkin**, etc. – for decoration

Instructions:

Beat the eggs in a large bowl and mix them with the yogurt.

Next, grate the cheese and add it to the batter along with the salt and the savory.

Start blending the mixture as you add some buckwheat flour.

Add as much flour as to reach the consistency of thick cake mixture.

Add the baking powder and the batter is ready!

Heat the oven to 180° C/ 356° F and bake the pastry until golden and when the toothpick comes out clean.

Halfway through the cooking, sprinkle the seeds on top so they don't burn.

Fast and Easy Balkan Bureks on a Skillet

Ingredients:

2 **Eggs**
1 1/2 cup **Milk**
1 1/2 cup **Gluten-free flour mix of choice**
A pinch of **Salt**
A pinch of **Baking soda**
1/2 cup **Feta cheese** (mashed)
Some **Butter**

Instructions:

First, whisk the eggs and mix them with the milk, the salt, and the baking soda.

Next, slowly start adding the flour as you continue to stir the mixture.

Finally, add the mashed feta cheese and stir once again to distribute it evenly.

Take a skillet or a frying pan with a lid and heat it on medium temperature.

Add some butter to grease the pan and let it melt completely.

Pour half of the batter in and put the lid on.

Leave the burek to get ready and flip it to cook on the other side. Add some more butter to grease the pastry and to make it even softer.

Repeat the process with the other half of the batter, but remember that if your pan is smaller, you can make more bureks with a smaller diameter.

Salty Cake with Blue Cheese

Ingredients:

1/2 cup **Rice flour**
3 **Eggs**
1 1/2 Tbsp. **Butter**
1/2 cup **Blue cheese** (mashed)
1 **Zucchini**
1 tsp. **Baking powder**

Instructions:

Start by heating the oven to 200° C/ 392° F, because the preparation of this recipe is very quick and easy!

Next, grate the zucchini in thin stripes.

Consecutively, blend all ingredients in a large container, and the batter for our salty cake is ready!

Take a flat baking pan and cover it with parchment paper.

Finally, pour the mixture in and bake for about 20 minutes (until fully cooked).

Voila!

My notes:

Salty Cake with Zucchini

Ingredients:

1 cup **Yogurt**
1/2 tsp. **Baking soda**
4 **Eggs**
1 1/2 cup **Rice flour**
1/2 cup **Feta cheese** (mashed)
1/2 cup **Dry stinging nettle**
1 **Zucchini**
Salt – to taste
Some **Olive oil**

Instructions:

First, mix the baking soda with the yogurt and stir.

When the dairy product starts to froth, mix it with the eggs, and the rice flour.

Blend the mixture completely, add the feta cheese, and stir with a fork.

Next, cut the zucchini in slices and start heating the oven to 200° C/ 392° F.

Now pour the cake mixture in a casserole and cover it with the zucchini slices.

Sprinkle some salt and pour the olive oil. You can add as much or as little fat as you like.

Bake the cake until fully cooked!

Cauliflower and Batata Quiche

Ingredients:

1 average **Cauliflower head**
1 large **Batata** (sweet potato)
3 **Eggs**
1 cup **Goat cheese**
1/2 cup **Yellow cheese**
2-3 Tbsps. **Olive oil**
Salt – to taste

Instructions:

First, mince the cauliflower in small pieces and cut the batata in thin slices.

Next, take a cake baking mold or a baking pan and grease it with some olive oil.

Now place one layer of cauliflower, cover it with sweet potato slices and sprinkle just a little bit of salt and some olive oil.

Continue adding more layers like this until you finish with the veggies. Be careful not to put too much salt because the two types of cheese will add more Sodium to the quiche.

Next, beat the eggs and grate the goat and the yellow cheese.

Blend everything well and pour the mixture on top of the dish.

Cover the quiche with tin foil and bake for about 45 minutes in a pre-heated oven at 200° C/ 392° F.

Turkish Leafy Green Pancakes (Kaygana)

Ingredients:

4 **Eggs**
1 cup **Gluten-free flour mix**
1 cup **Milk**
1/3 bunch of **Parsley**
1/3 bunch of **Fresh fennel**
3-4 **Scallion leaves**
1 tsp. **Salt**
1 tsp. **Butter** (or olive oil)

Instructions:

First, beat the eggs in a large bowl.

Next, add the flour, milk, and the salt, and blend completely with a whisk or a hand blender.

Next, cut the parsley (remove the stems), the fennel, and the scallion leaves in small pieces, and add them to the batter.

Finally, melt the butter in a non-stick frying pan and cook the pancakes on both sides. This quantity will yield about 4-5 pieces depending on the size of your pan.

You may need to add more butter (oil) for each pancake to make them softer and more delicious!

If you are using a regular skillet, this step is a must to prevent the dish from burning and sticking to the pan.

Enjoy!

GLUTEN-FREE SNACKS AND BITES

Very Easy Cheesy Bites (Low Carb)

Ingredients:

1 cup **Cream cheese**
1/2 cup **Soft feta cheese**
1 Tbsp. **Sour cream**
Some **Ground walnuts**
Some **Fresh fennel**

Instructions:

First, mash or grind the feta cheese (depending on the type you are using).

Next, simply blend with the cream cheese and the sour cream.

Finally, form the small cheesy balls and cover them with the ground walnuts and fennel.

Enjoy, and remember to store them in the fridge until consumption!

My notes:

Puffy Cheesy Bites

Ingredients:

1/2 cup **Water**
4 Tbsps. **Butter**
1/2 cup **Corn flour**
2 **Eggs**
4 Tbsps. **Grated feta cheese**
4 Tbsps. **Grated yellow cheese**
Spices of choice (fenugreek, pepper, caraway, savory, etc.) – to taste

Instructions:

First, place the water in a metal pot and heat it until it starts to simmer.

Add the butter, stir until it melts completely, and take it off the heat.

Now add the flour and continue to stir and blend until the mixture becomes fully homogenous, smooth and without any lumps.

Continue by adding the eggs along with the cheese and spices, and blend the batter once again.

At this point, you can start heating the oven to 190° C/ 374° F.

Next, take a baking pan and cover it parchment paper.

Scoop from the batter and form the bites with the desired shapes. If you feel inspired, you can use a piping bag to make the process less messy.

Bake the bites until fully cooked and golden.

Enjoy!

Cheese Balls with Corn

Ingredients:

2 **Potatoes** (boiled)
1 cup **Corn** (boiled or canned)
1/2 cup **Cream cheese spread**
1 Tbsp. **Milk**
1/2 cup **Fresh coriander** (minced)
2 Tbsps. **Corn flour**
2 Tbsps. **Gluten-free flour mix of choice**
Spices to taste – **Salt, Pepper, Savory, Basil, etc.**
2 cups **Gluten-free breadcrumbs**
Some **Butter**
3 1/2 Tbsps. **Grated cheese**

Instructions:

Place the corn and the corn flour in a chopper or a kitchen robot and blend them until homogeneous.

In another container, mash the potatoes until you have a nice and smooth puree.

Transfer the mixture into a large bowl and add the cream cheese, the potato puree, the milk, the coriander, and the spices.

Blend the ingredients well and add the breadcrumbs. Stir again to homogenize the mixture and we are ready to form the cheese balls.

Scoop from the mass and shape the bites as small spheres with the desired volume.

Next, cover them with the gated cheese and fry in the melted butter.

If you wish to avoid this procedure, bake the bites in a pre-heated oven until golden. You can place them in a pan with parchment paper to avoid burning the meal and the container.

Parsley Balls with White Sauce

Ingredients:

For the balls:
2 bunches of **Parsley**
1/2 cup **Feta cheese**
1 **Egg**
1 Tbsp. **Gluten-free flour mix**
Pepper – to taste
1 clove **Garlic**
3-4 Tbsps. **Olive oil**

For the sauce:
1 cup **Yogurt**
1 clove **Garlic**
A pinch of **Salt**
1-2 Tbsps. **Sesame tahini**

Instructions:

First, wash the parsley and remove its stems.
Mince the leaves in a kitchen chopper, and mix with the egg, 3 Tbsps. of the olive oil, and the flour.
Blend completely to homogenize the mixture.

Next, mash the feta cheese and the garlic clove, and add them to the mixture.

Stir again and the base for our parsley balls is ready. Remember, if it's too liquid, add more cheese.

Now heat the oven to the usual 180° C/ 356° F, take a baking tray and cover it with parchment paper. Sprinkle the remaining of the olive oil (1 Tbsp.) on top and it is time to form the balls.

Simply scoop from the mixture and shape them as you like.

Bake for about 10-15 minutes until fully cooked.

Meanwhile, we can make the sauce, which is also ridiculously easy.

Simply blend all ingredients in a kitchen chopper or a blender, and voila!

Vegetable Rissoles

Ingredients:

2 large **Potatoes**
2 large **Carrots**
2 fistfuls of **Shiitake mushrooms** (or regular buttons)
4 **Eggs**
3 Tbsps. **Corn flour** (non-GMO)
Salt – to taste
Some **Olive oil**

Instructions:

Cut the potatoes and the carrots in medium chunks and mince them in a kitchen chopper along with the mushrooms.

If you do not have such appliance, simply grate the veggies.

Beat the eggs in a bowl, and add the minced vegetables, but remember to squeeze the juice from them beforehand so that the rissoles won't become too moist.

Next, add the corn flour, the salt, and blend the ingredients well.

Now you can start heating the oven to the usual 180° C/ 356° F.

Take a baking tray and cover it with parchment paper, and grease it with the olive oil for extra protection.

Scoop from the mixture and form the rissoles on the pan.

Bake the dish until golden.

Voila!

My notes:

Salty Snacks with Walnuts

Ingredients:

2 cups **Gluten-free flour mix of choice**
2 **Eggs**
1/2 cup **Feta cheese**
1/2 cup **Ground walnuts**
1/2 cup **Butter** (soft)
Some **Salt and pepper** – to taste

Instructions:

First, grate the feta cheese and mix it with the butter.
Next, add the walnuts, and stir well.
If the mixture is not salty enough, add a little bit of salt and blend again.
Consecutively, add one cup of the flour and stir the mixture well.
Beat the eggs in another container, and add them to the main mixture along with the remaining flour.
Blend the dough one more time until it becomes fully homogeneous.
Cover the container with a towel and leave the dough to rest for about 15-20 minutes.
In the meantime, heat the oven to 180° C/ 356° F.
Now it is time to form the snacks!
Roll out the dough on a clean kitchen counter. Try to reach a thickness of about half a centimeter (0.2").
Next, cover it with some pure water.
Sprinkle some pepper on top or other spices you prefer and cut the dough layer in thin stripes.

Place the snacks in a baking tray covered with parchment paper and bake for about 20 minutes until golden and crunchy!

Corn Snacks with Cheese

Ingredients:

1 1/2 cup **Corn flour** (non-GMO)
1/2 cup **Feta cheese**
1/2 cup **Yellow cheese**
1/2 cup **Butter** (soft)
1 cup **Yogurt**
1 tsp. **Baking soda** (or baking powder)
1/2 tsp. **Salt**

Instructions:

Mix the baking soda with the yogurt and leave it to froth for a bit.

Grate the feta and the yellow cheese and simply blend all ingredients in a suitable container.

Heat the oven to the usual 180° C/ 356° F.

Meanwhile, we can form the snacks in a baking tray covered with parchment paper.

You can shape them as buns or use a piping bag and form some salty sticks.

It is totally up to you!

Bake the pastries until fully cooked and golden.

Gluten-free Bake Rolls

Ingredients:

1 **Egg**
2 Tbsps. **Grated cheese**
3-4 Tbsps. **Butter**
5 Tbsps. **Sesame flour** (full-fat)
2 Tbsps. **Rice flour**
Salt, oregano, garlic powder – to taste

Instructions:

Simply beat the egg and blend it with the remaining ingredients.

Spice the dough with the desired flavors.

Start forming small balls and arrange them in a baking pan covered with baking paper.

Press to flatten the snacks as thin as possible.

Next, heat the oven to 170° C/ 338° F and bake for about 12-13 minutes. When the bake rolls become golden, switch off the oven and leave the door open for 10 more minutes.

My notes:

Gluten-free Salty Snacks

Ingredients:

1 cup **Gluten-free flour mix of choice**
1/2 cup **Rice flour**
1 tsp. **Dry yeast** (gluten-free)
1 tsp. **Salt**
1/2 tsp. **Muscovado sugar**
1 **Egg**
5 1/2 Tbsps. **Olive oil**
2 Tbsps. **Coconut yogurt** (or regular cow yogurt)
1/2 cup **Warm water**

Instructions:

Mix the warm water with the dry yeast, the sugar, and stir well.
Next, add the two types of flour and blend again.
Leave the mixture to rise a bit.
Consecutively, add the remaining ingredients and stir nicely to homogenize the mixture.
Start forming the snacks with the desired shapes and place them in a baking pan covered with parchment paper.
Heat the oven to 40° C/ 104° F and place the snacks in for about 20 minutes for the dough to rise a bit more.
Finally, switch the temperature to 170° C/ 338° F and bake for about 40 more minutes until fully cooked.
Enjoy!

Gluten-free Salty Snacks with Lard

Ingredients:

For the dough:
1 cup **Lard** (soft)
2 **Egg yolks**
6 Tbsps. **Yogurt**
1 tsp. **Salt**
2 1/2 cups **Gluten-free flour mix**

For the filling:
2 **Egg whites**
1 cup **Feta cheese** (mashed)

For decoration:
1 **Egg**
Spices and seeds of choice – sunflower seeds, caraway, poppy seeds, etc.

Instructions:

First, beat the egg yolks and blend them with the lard and the salt.

Next, add the flour and stir until you reach soft elastic pliable dough.

If you need to, add more flour to get the desired consistency.

Next, prepare the filling by simply mixing and blending both ingredients completely.

Now place the dough on a kitchen counter (or a table) covered with gluten-free flour.

Roll it out in a thin layer – as thin as you can.

Next, cut it in squares with the desired size.

Place some of the filling inside each square and wrap it (or roll it) up.

Now you can start heating the oven to 180° C/ 356° F.

Meanwhile, arrange the snacks in a baking tray covered with parchment paper.

Finally, cover the pastries with the beaten egg and sprinkle some seeds and spices of your choice.

Bake until fully cooked and golden.

Homemade Nachos

Ingredients:

For the nachos:
1 cup **Corn flour**
1/2 cup **Gluten-free flour mix**
1/4 cup **Olive oil**
5-6 Tbsps. **Water**
1/2 tsp. **Salt**

For the sauce:
4 cloves **Garlic**
1/2 tsp. **Paprika**
Cayenne pepper – to taste
1 cup **Mayonnaise** (preferably homemade)
A pinch of **Salt**
1 tsp. **Tomato puree**
2 Tbsps. **Vinegar**

Instructions:

First, we start with the nachos.

Mix the corn flour, the gluten-free flour mix, the salt, and the olive oil in a suitable container.

Start blending the ingredients as you slowly add the water.

The goal is to reach soft and pliable non-sticky dough.

Transfer the mixture on a clean kitchen counter and continue to knead and blend the dough.

Next, roll it out to the desired thickness (about 0.5 cm).

At this point, you can start heating the oven to 180° C/ 356° F.

Consecutively, cut the dough in the desired shapes.

Now transfer the nachos in a baking tray covered with parchment paper.

Bake for about 5-6 minutes or until fully cooked and nicely crunchy.

Next, we can make the sauce. You can use whatever gluten-free option you prefer, but this one is very delicious!

Mince the garlic cloves in a kitchen chopper or a garlic press.

Mix it with the mayonnaise and all the remaining ingredients.

Stir and blend until the mixture is fully homogeneous.

And that's it! So easy and yummy!

Homemade Avocado Mayonnaise

Ingredients:

1 large **Avocado** (fully ripe)
1/2 bunch of **Parsley**
3 **Eggs** (boiled)
3-4 cloves **Garlic**
Soft feta cheese (or cream cheese) – to taste
Lemon juice – to taste

Instructions:

This is one a little unorthodox mayonnaise recipe that I think you will love!

It is very simple to make and you can adjust the quantities of the ingredients according to your preferences.

All you need to do is combine all substances in a blender, kitchen robot, or a chopper and blend them until fully homogeneous. Remember to remove the stems from the parsley to make the consistency smoother.

Add as much cheese as you wish to match your preferred taste!

And that's it! So easy, and yet – so tasty!

My notes:

Homemade Avocado Mayonnaise (Vegan)

Ingredients:

2 large **Avocados** (fully ripe)
2 1/2 Tbsps. **Lemon juice**
1/4 tsp. **Apple cider vinegar**
3 Tbsps. **Extra virgin olive oil**
1 Tbsp. **Water**
Salt – to taste
7-8 **Tarragon leaves**

Instructions:

Pit the avocados and cut them in cubes.

Transfer them into the kitchen robot (or a chopper) along with the remaining ingredients.

Stir and blend until you reach a homogeneous mass.

Pour the mayonnaise in a glass jar, seal it and place it in the fridge overnight to develop its taste!

Easy right!

My notes:

Very Simple Salty Sticks

Ingredients:

1 **Egg**
1 Tbsp. **Olive oil**
Salt – to taste
5-6 Tbsps. **Rice flour**

Instructions:

Simply blend the ingredients and transfer the mixture in a piping bag or a cooking syringe.

Spritz the mixture into a baking tray covered with parchment paper to form the salty sticks.

Bake in a pre-heated oven at 180° C/ 356° F for about 15 minutes.

Voila!

My notes:

Salty Corn Sticks

Ingredients:

1 1/2 cup **Corn flour** (non-GMO)
1 cup **Lukewarm water**
1 **Egg**
5-6 Tbsps. **Butter** (soft)
1 tsp. **Salt** (Himalayan or sea salt)
1 tsp. **Baking powder**

Instructions:

Blend all ingredients well until you reach a homogeneous mass.

Leave the dough to rest for about 30 minutes.

Next, start heating the oven to 230° C/ 446° F.

Transfer the dough into a piping bag and commence forming the salty sticks on a baking tray covered with parchment paper.

Bake for about 15 minutes and that's it!

Easy-peasy! Right?

My notes:

GLUTEN-FREE MUFFINS

Salty Muffins I

Ingredients:

1/2 cup **Rice flour**
2 **Eggs**
2 tsps. **Baking powder**
1/2 cup **Feta cheese** (mashed)
1 cup **Yogurt**
3 Tbsps. **Butter**
A pinch of **Salt**
A pinch of **Muscovado sugar** (or coconut sugar)

Instructions:

Start heating the oven to 150° C/ 302° F.

In the meantime, simply blend all ingredients well with a hand mixer or a blender.

If you wish to leave larger chunks of the cheese, add them after you have homogenized the batter.

Pour the mixture in your favorite non-stick muffin molds and bake until fully cooked and golden.

Due to the lower temperature, it may take a bit more time, but it is worth it!

Salty Muffins II (with Feta Cheese)

Ingredients:

1 cup **Yogurt**
1 tsp. **Baking soda**
A pinch of **Salt**
2 **Eggs**
3 Tbsps. **Butter**
3-4 Tbsps. **Feta cheese** (mashed)
1/2 cup **Corn flour**
3 1/2 Tbsps. **Buckwheat flour**

Instructions:

First, as usual, mix the baking soda with the yogurt and wait for it to start frothing.

In the meantime, you can start heating the oven to 150° C/ 302° F.

Next, blend all ingredients well until you reach a nice homogeneous mass.

Pour the batter in the muffin molds and bake until fully cooked (when the toothpick comes out clean).

My notes:

Salty Muffins III

Ingredients:

3 **Eggs**
1/2 cup **Gluten-free oat meal flour**
1/2 cup **Flax seed flour**
3 Tbsps. **Yogurt**
Spices (honey garlic, savory, chili pepper) – to taste
Some **Grated cheese** – optional
Some **Coconut butter** – for the muffin molds

Instructions:

The preparation is very simple and easy!

Beat the eggs in a large bowl and blend them with the flour, yogurt, and the spices.

Take your favorite muffin molds and grease them with some coconut butter.

Next, pour the batter in and cover the pastries with some grated cheese, if you desire.

Heat the oven to 150° C - 160° C / 302° F - 320° F and bake until fully cooked.

My notes:

-----------------------------   -----------------------------
----

Salty Muffins IV (with Cream Cheese)

Ingredients:

2 **Eggs**
1/2 cup **Cream cheese** (or cottage cheese)
1/2 tsp. **Salt** (ground sea salt or Himalayan)
1/2 tsp. **Baking powder**
2 Tbsps. **Chickpea flour**
1/2 cup **Coconut milk** (warm)
1/2 cup **Rice flour**
Some **Feta cheese** – to taste

Instructions:

This recipe is very quick and easy, so you can start by heating the oven to 180° C/ 356° F.

Next, simply blend all ingredients (except the feta cheese) in a bowl and stir with a hand mixer (or a hand blender).

After that, mash the feta cheese, add it to the batter, and stir with a fork.

Pour the mixture in a muffin tin and bake until fully cooked (about 30-35 minutes).

My notes:

Salty Muffins V (with Powerful Healing Spices)

Ingredients:

1 1/2 cup **Yogurt**
1 Tbsp. **Baking soda**
3 **Eggs**
1 tsp. **Salt**
1/2 cup **Feta cheese**
1/2 cup **Butter** (melted)
2 Tbsps. **Black cumin**
2 Tbsps. **Turmeric**
1 1/2 cup **Gluten-free flour mix**
Some seeds of choice – **poppy, sunflower, pumpkin**, etc. – for decoration

Instructions:

First, mix the yogurt with the baking soda and let it froth for a bit.

Next, add the eggs, the salt, and blend nicely.

Mash the feta cheese and add it to the batter along with the butter and the spices.

Now add the flour and blend the mixture once again until fully homogeneous.

Start heating the oven to 180° C/ 356° F.

Pour the batter in muffin baking molds, sprinkle some of the seed mix, and cook for about 30 minutes.

Vegetable Muffins

Ingredients:

1 cup **Chickpea flour**
1/2 cup **Rice flour**
1/2 cup **Olive oil**
2 tsps. **Baking powder**
2 **Eggs**
1 cup **Yogurt**
2 **Carrots**
2 fistfuls of **Spinach**
Salt – to taste

Instructions:

First, we need to prepare the veggies.

Steam them until they soften and blend them in a kitchen chopper or a robot.

Next, mix both types of flour in a bowl along with the baking powder.

In another container, beat the eggs and blend them with the vegetable puree, the salt, and the olive oil.

Combine both mixtures and stir with a hand mixture (or a blender) to homogenize the mixture.

Heat the oven to 160° C/ 320° F and bake the muffins in your favorite baking tray until fully cooked and golden.

Enjoy!

Muffins with Cream Cheese and Zucchinis (Low Carb)

Ingredients:

2 average **Zucchinis**
1 cup **Cream cheese**
1 average **Carrot**
1/2 bunch of **Fennel**
1 cup **Bacon**
4 **Eggs**
1/2 cup **Cheese**
Salt and pepper – to taste

Instructions:

First, grate the zucchinis (or mince them in a kitchen chopper), mix them with some salt, and place them in a colander to secret their juice.

Next, mince the fennel and mix it with the eggs and the other spices.

Grate the carrot and add it to the mixture.

Now squeeze any remaining liquid from the zucchinis (as much as possible) and add them to the batter as well.

Grate the cheese, dice the bacon, and transfer them to the mixture.

Stir and blend the batter completely and we are ready for the final part.

Heat the oven to 200° C/ 392° F and pour the mixture into a muffin tin (usually with about 12 muffin cups).

Bake the dishes for about 30-40 minutes until fully cooked.

Potato Muffins

Ingredients:

5-6 medium **Potatoes**
A fistful of **Diced sausage** (preferably bio or homemade)
3 **Eggs**
1/3 cup **Corn flour** (non-GMO)
3-4 Tbsps. **Butter**
3-4 Tbsps. **Feta cheese** (mashed)
Spices of your choice – to taste

Instructions:

First, boil the potatoes completely, strain them from the water and mash them.

Add your desired spices and stir well.

Next, beat the eggs, and mix them with the potato puree, the butter, the cheese, and the corn flour.

Blend the mixture completely until it becomes fully homogeneous.

Now heat the oven to 200° C/ 392° F.

Divide the muffin mix into some baking molds and bake until golden.

Easy peasy, right?

Egg Muffins with Mushrooms (Low Carb)

Ingredients:

3 **Carrots** (small)
1/2 **Zucchini**
1 **Green pepper**
Several **Oyster mushrooms** (or common button mushrooms)
9-12 **Eggs**
1/2 bunch of **Fresh parsley**
1/2 bunch of **Fresh fennel**
Salt and Pepper – to taste
Some **Coconut butter**

Instructions:

Start heating the oven to 180° C/ 356° F.

Next, clean and dice all of the vegetables – the carrots, zucchini, pepper, mushrooms, parsley, and fennel.

In another container, beat the eggs and blend them with the veggies.

Add the spices you desire and stir nicely one more time.

Now we have the filling for our healthy (and low carb) muffins.

Take your favorite muffin mold (with 12 cups) and grease it with the coconut butter.

Fill the cups with the vegetable mixture and place them in the oven.

Bake until fully cooked – the top of the muffins will have a nice crunchy crust! Enjoy!

OTHER GLUTEN-FREE MEALS AND SIDE DISHES

Stuffed Peppers with Buckwheat

Ingredients:

1/2 cup **Buckwheat**
1 **Onion bulb**
3 **Carrots**
1 **Egg**
3 Tbsps. **Olive oil**
1/2 cup **Peas** (canned)
4 1/2 Tbsps. **Cottage cheese**
1/2 bunch of **Fresh parsley**
1/2 bunch of **Fresh fennel**
Salt and Pepper – to taste
Some Hot water – to cover the buckwheat
Several **Red peppers**

Instructions:

First, place the buckwheat in a cup or a bowl and cover it with the hot water. Leave it aside to soften for an hour.

In the meantime, we will prepare the other ingredients.

Peel and dice the onion.

Grate the carrots or mince them in a kitchen chopper.

Beat the egg in a cup, and strain the peas from their juice from the can.

Mince the green spices as well.

When the buckwheat becomes nicely soft, it is time to strain it from the water.

Next, add the onion, the carrot shreds, the eggs, the peas, olive oil, and the spices.

Blend the ingredients well and the stuffing for our peppers is ready!

You can start heating the oven to 200° C/ 392° F at this point.

Take each red pepper, wash it, cut it in half, and remove the seeds.

Fill the red veggies with the stuffing and place them in a baking pan.

Pour a little bit of water at the bottom to prevent from the peppers to stick to the container and burn.

Roast the meal for about 30 minutes until fully cooked.

Stuffed Zucchini with Onion Sauce

Ingredients:

1 **Zucchini**
4-5 Tbsps. **Diced bacon**
2 Tbsps. **Grated parmesan**

For the sauce:
2 cups **Yogurt**
3-4 cloves **Garlic**
1 tsp. **Salt**
A bunch of **Fresh fennel**
2-3 Tbsps. **Olive oil**

Instructions:

This recipe is very easy and simple.

Cut the zucchini in half. Scoop some of the pulp and blend it with the diced bacon.

Fill the vegetable with the stuffing and sprinkle the cheese on top.

Heat the oven to 200° C/ 392° F and bake for about 5-6 minutes.

Meanwhile, we can prepare the sauce.

Mince the garlic cloves in a kitchen chopper and cut the fennel leaves in small pieces.

Now blend all the ingredients well and that's it!

Vegetable Casserole

Ingredients:

1 **Zucchini**
6 **Eggs**
1/2 cup **Goat cheese** (or feta cheese)
2 **Green peppers**
6 Tbsps. **Rice flour**
3-4 Tbsps. **Olive oil**
A pinch of **Stinging nettle powder**
Fresh fennel – to taste
Salt – to taste

Instructions:

You can start by heating the oven to 200° C/ 392° F.

Next, cut the zucchini in slices and arrange then at the bottom of a casserole.

Sprinkle some salt and pepper to spice the veggies a bit.

You can oil the container with some butter or olive oil beforehand, if you like.

Next, mash the goat cheese and mix it with the eggs.

Blend the ingredients well and add the rice flour. Stir again to homogenize the mixture completely.

Consecutively, cut the peppers in small pieces and add them to the cheese and eggs.

Stir one more time, and pour the mixture on top of the zucchini slices.

Spread it nicely to fully cover the vegetables.

Next, pour the olive oil on top.

Finally, mince the fennel finely, and sprinkle it on top of the dish along with the stinging nettle and some more salt and pepper, if you wish.

Put the casserole in the oven and roast until fully cooked and golden.

Bon Appetite!

My notes:

Chickpea "Meatballs"

Ingredients:

1 1/2 cup **Chickpeas** (boiled or canned)
5-6 Tbsps. **Peas** (canned)
2 **Eggs**
1 **Lemon**
A bunch of **Parsley**
5 Tbsps. **Olive oil** (plus, a little bit more for the baking pan)
A pinch of **Turmeric powder**
Salt – to taste
Some **Corn flour** (non-GMO)

Instructions:

First, start heating the oven to 180° C/ 356° F.

Strain the chickpeas from the can, mix them with the peas, and mash them thoroughly.

Alternatively, you can use a kitchen chopper or a robot to make your life easier.

Next, mince the parsley finely and add it to the legumes.

Squeeze the juice from the lemon, and add it to the mix.

Consecutively, add the eggs, the olive oil, the spices, and blend all ingredients completely.

If the mixture becomes too runny, add more peas to make the consistency thicker.

Next, form the "meatballs" and cover them with corn flour.

Take a suitable baking pan and cover it with some oil.

Arrange the balls inside, and roast them for about 20 minutes.

Easy peasy!

Chicken Meatballs

Ingredients:

1 1/2 cup **Chicken fillet**
1 **Carrot**
2 **Eggs**
1 **Lemon**
Some **Parsley** – to taste
Salt and pepper – to taste
1 Tbsp. **Corn flour** (non-GMO)
1 Tbsp. **Butter** (soft)

Instructions:

First, boil the chicken meat, strain it, and cut it in small pieces.

Grate the carrot or mince it in a kitchen chopper.

Cut the parsley leaves as well.

Next, beat the eggs in a bowl and blend them with the corn flour.

Add the remaining ingredients and stir again to homogenize the mixture.

Now heat the oven to 180° C/ 356° F.

Finally, form small meatballs from the mixture and arrange then in a baking pan covered with parchment paper.

Bake until golden and bon appetite!

Meatballs with Tartar Sauce (Low Carb)

Ingredients:

For the meatballs:
2 cups **Minced meat** (it could be 1/2 pork, 1/2 beef)
1 **Onion bulb**
1/2 cup **Cheese**
5 **Pickled cucumbers** (dill pickles)
4-5 Tbsps. **Canned mushrooms** (sliced)
A bunch of **Parsley**
Salt, pepper, cumin - to taste

For the sauce:
4 **Pickled cucumbers**
1 Tbsp. **Mustard** (Dijon)
1 Tbsp. **Mayonnaise** (preferably homemade)
2 cloves **Garlic**
1 **Scallion**
Salt – to taste

Instructions:

It is best to start preparing the dish the day before.

Mince the onion in a kitchen chopper, or if you feel brave enough – grate it.

Repeat with the parsley (remove any stalks beforehand) and the mushrooms.

Dice the cucumbers and the cheese.

Now combine all the ingredients in a bowl (with the minced meat and the spices) and blend completely.

Cover the container with kitchen foil and leave the mixture overnight in the fridge.

The next day, stir and knead the mixture again and form the meatballs.

Roast them on the grill unit fully cooked.

Now we can start making the sauce.

Mince the garlic, the onion and the pickles in a kitchen chopper.

Transfer the veggies into a bowl and add the remaining ingredients.

Stir and blend completely. Cover the container with kitchen foil and place it in the fridge for about an hour for the flavors to fully develop.

Final step – serve and enjoy!

Quinoa "Risotto"

Ingredients:

For the "risotto":
3-4 cups **Vegetable broth**
1 **Onion bulb**
1 Tbsp. **Olive oil**
2 Tbsps. **Butter**
1 cup **Quinoa**
3 1/2 Tbsps. **White wine**
1/4 – 1/2 cup **Beetroot juice**
1 **Bay leaf**
Several stalks **Fresh thyme**
2 bulbs **Beetroot** – boiled

For dressing:
1 **Apple**
1 1/2 Tbsp. **Butter**
2 Tbsps. **Coconut sugar**
3 1/2 Tbsps. **Water**
1 Tbsp. **Balsamic vinegar**
2 Tbsps. **Parmesan**
1/2 cup **Goat cheese**
Salt and **Pepper** – to taste

Instructions:

First, dice the onion, and melt the butter in a deep pan (or a large saucepan).

Next, add the olive oil, just a little bit of water, and stew the onion on low heat until transparent.

Now add the quinoa, and stir until it softens and becomes transparent as well.

Consecutively, add the wine, the beetroot juice, the bay leaf, and the thyme.

Continue to stir and blend the ingredients until the liquid evaporates and the mixture becomes thicker.

Next, start slowly adding the vegetable broth until it submerges the risotto.

Leave the mixture to simmer for about 15 minutes.

In the meantime, dice the beetroot bulbs, and after the time is up – add them to the dish.

Let the meal cook for 10 more minutes, and in the meantime we can prepare the dressing.

Slice the apple in thin segments, and melt the butter in a metal pot along with the sugar.

Next, add the apple slices, and wait for them to caramelize a bit.

After that, add the water and the balsamic vinegar, and stir well.

When the mixture becomes thicker, add some salt.

Finally, arrange the dish by garnishing it with some of grated parmesan, the caramel apples, mashed goat cheese, and some salt and pepper to taste.

Voila!

Imperial Lunch

Ingredients:

3-4 Tbsps. **Black rice**
1 **Penny bun** (Boletus edulis)
1 **Egg**
1 Tbsp. **Olive oil**
Salt and pepper – to taste
1 **Bay leaf**
Some **Coconut butter**

Instructions:

Place the rice, the mushroom, the bay leaf, and the salt in a metal pot and cover them with water.

Heat the mixture on low temperature and boil for about 20 minutes.

Next, remove the boletus and strain the rice.

Mix the black grains with the pepper and the olive oil.

Heat a non-stick pan with some coconut butter and cook the whole egg without scrambling it.

Serve the dish as you place the egg on top of the mushroom and the rice on the side. Bon appetite!

"Risotto" With Eggs

Ingredients:

For 1 serving:
1 **Egg**
1 cup **Basmati rice**
2 Tbsps. **Peanut butter** (or sesame tahini)
1 tsp. **Butter**
1 clove **Garlic**
2 Tbsps. **Ground ginger root**
1 cup **Minced leek**
2 tsps. **Soy sauce** (organic)
Salt – to taste

Instructions:

First, soak the rice in some clean water overnight.

On the next day, strain the grains, wash the rice thoroughly, and boil it on low heat until fully cooked.

Next, as we are waiting for the grains to cool down, we can prepare the spices.

Heat the butter in a frying pan and add the peanut butter, the minced garlic, and the ginger.

Stir until the veggies caramelize and get a nice golden color.

Strain them from the fat and leave them aside to cool down a bit.

Next, place the minced leek in the pan and cook on low temperature until it softens (about 10 minutes). Again, if the butter is not enough you can add some more, but remember that the leek absorbs a lot of it and the dish might become too greasy.

Next, turn up the temperature and add the strained boiled rice.

Strain and spice with some salt.

Consecutively, break the egg on top and let it cook until the egg white coagulates (you can leave the yolk semi-cooked).

Finally, serve garnished with the caramelized veggies we prepared earlier.

Note: you can adjust the quantities of the ingredients to scale up and down and match your preferred size of one serving!

Cauliflower Moussaka

Ingredients:

1 large **Cauliflower**
3 **Onion bulbs**
4 **Tomatoes**
1 cup **Basmati rice**
3 **Eggs**
1 cup **Yogurt**
2 Tbsps. **Chickpea flour**
Some **Ghee**
Some **Coconut butter**
Spices (salt, pepper, cumin, parsley) – to taste

Instructions:

First, wash the cauliflower and chop off its florets.

Blanch them in some boiling salty water for about 10 minutes.

Next, remove the florets from the saline and cut them in small pieces. Remember not to throw away the stock – we will need it later on in the recipe!

Spice the cauliflower "rice" with some cumin.

Next, dice the onion and cook it in 1 Tbsp. ghee and 1 Tbsp. coconut butter until it softens.

Consecutively, add the Basmati and stir until it becomes transparent.

Sprinkle some salt and take the dish off the heat.

Dice 2 tomatoes and the parsley in small pieces, and add them to the rice.

Add the cauliflower, spice with some pepper and stir well to blend the mixture.

Transfer everything into a baking pan and add one cup of the cauliflower stock.

Heat the oven to 180° C/ 356° F.

Meanwhile, cut the remaining 2 tomatoes in slices and place them on top of the moussaka.

Bake the dish until fully cooked.

And finally – the topping.

Blend the yogurt with the eggs and the chickpea flour.

Pour the mixture on top of the moussaka and let it cook for several more minutes until golden!

Zucchini "Pasta" with Bolognese Sauce (Low Carb)

Ingredients:

For the "pasta":
1-2 **Zucchinis**
Spiralizer

For the sauce:
1 1/2 cup **Minced meat**
1 **Onion bulb**
2 cloves **Garlic**
1 **Carrot**
2 stalks **Celery**
1 **Red pepper**
2 cups **Tomatoes**
A bunch of **Fresh basil**
1 Tbsp. **Tomato puree**
1/2 cup **White wine**
Salt and **Pepper** – to taste
Some **Olive oil**

Instructions:

First, we will start with the sauce since it takes a bit more time than the vegetable pasta.

Remove the stalks of the basil and mince the leaves in small pieces.

Dice the garlic cloves, the onion, the red pepper, and the carrot.

Next, blanch the celery stalks in some boiling salty water until they soften.

Strain them from the saline, and dice them as well. Note: do not throw away the hot saline – we will need it later on in the recipe!

Take a deep pan and pour some olive oil in it.

Heat the fatty substance and add the minced meat.

As you cook the meat, add the onion and the garlic, and stir continuously.

In a few minutes, add the remaining minced veggies along with the tomato puree.

Continue to cook the mixture on low temperature while you cut the tomatoes in medium pieces.

Next, add them in the pan along with the wine and leave the sauce to simmer until it is fully cooked and blended.

Leave it aside to cool down a bit.

Meanwhile, we can make the pasta.

Use the spiralizer to cut the zucchinis in thin stripes.

If you do not have such appliance, you can use a potato peeler instead.

Heat the saline we used earlier in the recipe until it starts to simmer.

Place the zucchini pasta in and let it cook for about 4-5 minutes until it softens.

Finally, strain the veggies and garnish them with the sauce.

Bon appetite!

Summer Zucchini Frittata (Low Carb)

Ingredients:

3 1/2 cups **Zucchinis**
4-5 **Eggs**
3 1/2 Tbsps. **Milk**
1 **Onion bulb**
2 cloves **Garlic**
1/2 cup **Yellow cheese**
A bunch of **Fresh parsley**
2-3 Tbsps. **Olive oil**
Salt – to taste

Instructions:

First, prepare the zucchinis by cutting them in semi-circles.

After that, dice the onion and the garlic cloves.

Next, pour some olive oil in a pan and fry them for a minute.

Add the zucchinis and let them cook for 6-7 minutes on medium heat until they soften.

In the meantime, grate the cheese and cut the parsley in small pieces.

Beat the eggs in a bowl and blend them with the milk and the salt.

Add the grated cheese, the leafy green, and the half-cooked zucchinis.

Heat the oven to 180° C/ 356° F.

Next, pour the mixture in a baking mold (with about 8" diameter) and bake for about half an hour. Voilà!

Mini Veggie Muffin Omelettes (Low Carb)

Ingredients:

6 **Eggs**
3 **Carrots**
1/2 head **Broccoli**
Several **Cherry tomatoes**
Some **Yellow cheese** – to taste
Spices (salt, pepper, turmeric, caraway) – to taste

Instructions:

First, beat the eggs in a bowl and blend them with the spices.

Next, mince the vegetables in small pieces and dice the cheese in tiny cubes.

Start heating the oven to 180° C/ 356° F.

Take a muffin tin and divide the veggies and the cheese into each cup. Pour the eggs on top and bake the omelettes for about 20-25 minutes.

If your oven is fan-assisted, feel free to use this option for this recipe.

My notes:

Cream Cheese Omelette (Low Carb)

Ingredients:

6 **Eggs**
1/2 cup **Cream cheese**
1 cup **Feta cheese**
1/2 bunch of **Parsley**
Some **Fennel and pepper** – to taste

Instructions:

Mince the leafy greens in small pieces and mash the feta cheese.

Beat the eggs in a bowl and blend them with the remaining ingredients.

You can use a whisk, a hand mixer or a fork.

Heat the oven to 220° C/ 428° F.

Pour the egg omelette mixture in a baking pan covered with parchment paper.

Bake the dish for about 15 minutes until fully cooked.

Enjoy!

My notes:

Zucchini & Chicken Rolls (Low Carb)

Ingredients:

1 **Zucchini**
1-2 **Grilled chicken breasts**
1/2 cup **Cheese**
2-3 Tbsps. **Olive oil**
Salt – to taste

Instructions:

First, cut the zucchini in thin slices.

Next, heat the oven to 200° C/ 392° F.

Now transfer the zucchini slices in a baking tray and cover them with some salt and olive oil.

Roast the veggies until they soften.

In the meantime, grate the cheese and shred the chicken breasts with forks (or cut them in small pieces).

When the zucchinis are ready, take half of the grated cheese and sprinkle it inside the vegetable slices. Repeat with the chicken meat, roll the zucchinis to wrap the stuffing and fixate the bites with toothpicks.

Sprinkle the remaining of the cheese on top and bring the rolls back in the oven.

Roast the dish until golden.

Bon appetite!

Zucchini & Cheese Rolls (Low Carb)

Ingredients:

2 **Zucchinis**
1/2 cup **Cream cheese**
2-3 Tbsps. **Sour cream**
Salt, pepper, fennel, honey garlic – to taste
Some **Yellow cheese** – to cover the dish

Instructions:

First, cut the zucchinis in thin slices.

Next, mix the cream cheese with the sour cream, the spices, and blend them well.

Cover the vegetable slices with the filling and roll them gently.

Now grate the cheese – the quantity will depend on the area it needs to cover and your personal preferences.

Arrange the rolls in a baking pan covered with parchment paper, and sprinkle the grated cheese on top.

Bake in a pre-heated oven (at 180° C/ 356° F) for about 20 minutes.

Enjoy!

My notes:

Zucchini & Cream Cheese Roll (Low Carb)

Ingredients:

For the roll:
2 **Zucchinis**
2 **Carrots**
4 **Eggs**
1/2 cup **Cottage cheese**
1/2 bunch of **Fennel**
1/2 tsp. **Salt**
Garlic powder and pepper – to taste

For the filling:
1/2 cup **Cream cheese**
Olives

Instructions:

First, grate the zucchinis (or mince them in a chopper), spice them with some salt and place them in a colander to secret their juice.

Next, beat the eggs in a bowl and blend them with the spices.

Squeeze the liquid from the zucchinis as much as possible and add them to the main batter.

Grate (or mince) the carrots as well, and add them to the mixture.

Take a baking tray and cover it with moist wrinkled parchment paper.

Pour the batter in and bake in a pre-heated oven at 200° C/ 392° F for about half an hour.

In the meantime, pit the olives and mince them in small pieces.

Next, take the dish out of the oven and leave it to cool down a bit.

Now spread the cream cheese on top and sprinkle the olive bits.

Finally, use the baking paper to roll the zucchini layer to form the dish.

Cut in slices, serve and enjoy!

Rhodopean Potato Dish (Patatnik)

Ingredients:

6-7 average **Potatoes**
1 **Onion bulb**
1 **Egg**
Spices (salt, pepper, mint) – to taste
2-3 Tbsps. **Olive oil**
1 1/2 Tbsp. **Gluten free flour mix**

Instructions:

First, grate the potatoes and the onion bulb. Alternatively, you can mince them in a kitchen chopper.

Next, squeeze out as much of their juice as possible.

Now add the egg and the spices, and blend completely.

Next, heat the olive oil in a frying pan (with a lid).

Sprinkle the flour on top to cover the whole appliance.

Cook the flour for about a minute.

Scoop some of the potato mixture and place in the pan. Press with a spatula to flatten the dish. Aim for about half an inch width.

Put the lid on and let the patatnik cook for about 5-6 minutes on medium heat. Check to see if the bottom of the dish had become nicely golden and crunchy. Then, flip it and cook on the other side. This time you don't need to put the lid on so that the excess water can evaporate and leave the dish with a nice golden crust.

Repeat the process for the remaining of the batter – the yield will depend on the size of your pan and the quantity of the mixture.

Feel free to garnish the patatnik with some grated feta or yellow cheese (or both!) while it's still hot. Yum!

Stuffed Potatoes with Bacon

Ingredients:

6 large **Potatoes**
1 cup **Bacon** (boiled smoked)
1 cup **Yellow cheese**
4 Tbsps. **Butter** (soft)
1 cup **Cottage cheese**
A bunch of **Fennel**
Salt and **Pepper** – to taste

Instructions:

First, boil the potatoes whole with their skin in some salty water.

In the meantime, cut 12 slices of the bacon and mince the remaining quantity in small pieces.

Mix the diced bacon with the cottage cheese in a bowl.

Next, grate the yellow cheese and add it to the mix along with the butter.

Spice the mixture with some salt, pepper, and minced fennel.

Stir and blend completely until you have a homogeneous mass.

Now, when the potatoes are fully cooked, strain them from the saline and leave them to cool down.

Cut them in equal halves and scoop some of their insides.

Fill them with the cheese mixture and place a slice of bacon at the top.

Next, heat the oven to 200° C/ 392° F and bake the dish for about 15-20 minutes.

My notes:

Stuffed Pumpkin with Meat

Ingredients:

1 **Pumpkin** (about 3 pounds)
1/2 cup **Boiled buckwheat**
2 Tbsps. **Butter**
1 cup **Meat** (fillet, minced meat or bacon)
1 head **Garlic**
1 **Onion bulb**
1/2 cup **Water**
Salt and **Pepper** – to taste
Some **Olive oil**

Instructions:

First, cut the cap of the pumpkin, scoop out the seeds, and spice it with some salt and pepper.

Next, heat the oven to 200° C/ 392° F and bake the pumpkin for about an hour.

The goal is for the insides of the squash to be nicely soft while it maintains its shape.

When the pumpkin cools down a bit, scoop some of its insides to make space for the stuffing. Try to leave at least an inch of the pumpkin walls and remember to keep the pulp.

Consecutively, we can start preparing the stuffing.

Strain the buckwheat thoroughly to remove as much water as possible.

Cook it in some hot butter for several minutes.

Next, dice the onion and the garlic cloves and cut the meat in small pieces.

Heat some olive oil (or butter) in a pan and caramelize the onion and the garlic.

Add the meat chunks and cook for about 10 minutes.

Next, add the pumpkin flesh that we scooped out, the buckwheat, and blend completely.

Now, fill the squash with the stuffing, bring the water (1/2 cup) to boil, pour it in and put the cap on top.

Bring the dish back in the oven for one more hour or until fully cooked.

Vegan Romanian Polenta (Mamaliga)

Ingredients:

1 cup **Corn meal** (non-GMO)
4 cups **Vegan milk** (almond, rice, coconut, etc.)
1 stalk **Fresh oregano**
1 tsp. **Turmeric**
1/2 cup **Olive oil**
1 Tbsp. **Sesame tahini**
Salt and **Pepper** – to taste
Some **Ground Nuts** - optional

Instructions:

Place the milk in a metal pot along with the spices, and bring it to boil.

Start slowly adding the corn meal in the port as you continuously stir with a whisk.

Continue blending the ingredients until you reach the desired consistency.

Next, add the olive oil and the tahini, and spice the dish with some salt and pepper.

Garnish with some ground nuts of choice, if you desire.

Gluten-free Gypsy Schnitzel

Ingredients:

3 **Red peppers**
4 **Pork schnitzels** (thinned pork meat)
2 cups **Beef broth**
1 large **Onion bulb**
1 clove **Garlic**
1/2 cup **Tomato puree**
5-6 Tbsps. **Corn flour** (non-GMO)
Salt, pepper, paprika – to taste
2 Tbsps. **Butter**
Some **Fresh parsley** (for decoration)

Instructions:

First, let's prepare the veggies!

Cut the onion, the garlic, and the peppers in medium pieces.

Next, spice the schnitzels with the salt, pepper, and the paprika and cover them fully with half of the corn flour.

Take a frying pan and heat the butter.

Place the spiced meat in and cook until it becomes nicely golden.

Then, (especially if the meat is not tender enough), wrap it in some cooking foil and place it in the oven, heated to 170° C/ 338° F.

Meanwhile, place the minced onion and garlic in the hot butter left from the meat and cook until caramelized. If the fat is not enough, add a bit more butter or olive oil.

Next, add the peppers and some salt to taste.

Cook the veggies until they soften a little bit.

Now gently separate the fried peppers from the hot fat. Simply push them to one end of the pan and tilt the container so that the melted butter drains down the other end.

Place the remaining of the corn flour in the hot fat, and fry it until it thickens. Again, if the butter is not enough, simply add some more!

When the flour is ready and fully cooked, stir the whole mixture and add the tomato puree, and the beef broth.

Leave the dish to simmer on low heat for about 10 more minutes.

If it becomes too thick in the process, just add a little bit of warm water.

Finally, serve the schnitzels garnished with the sauce on top and some minced parsley leaves for splendor!

My notes:

Gourmet Appetizer with Salmon, Lentils, and Quinoa

Ingredients:

For the salmon:
4 **Salmon fillets**
1 Tbsp. **Brown sugar** (or Muscovado, coconut sugar, etc.)
1 tsp. **Curry**
1 tsp. **Pepper**
2 cloves **Garlic**
1/2 **Star anise**
1/2 tsp. **Cumin**
1 tsp. **Black sesame seeds**
1-2 Tbsps. **Olive oil**

For the lentils:
1 cup **Lentils** (soaked)
1 cup **Celery roots**
2 cloves **Garlic**
1/2 cup **Olive oil**
1/2 cup **Rice vinegar**
1/2 cup **Soy sauce**
1/2 cup **Agave syrup**
1 tsp. **Smoked red pepper**
2 cups **Vegetable broth**

For the quinoa:
1 cup **Quinoa**
Some **Rice vinegar** – to taste
Some **Olive oil** – to taste

Spices (salt, pepper, nutmeg, parsley, tarragon) – to taste

For the red cabbage:
1/2 cup **Red cabbage**
1 Tbsp. **Honey**
Balsamic vinegar and Olive oil – to taste

Instructions:

We start this long, but delicious gourmet recipe by boiling the quinoa in some salty water for about 10-15 minutes.

In the meantime, cut the green spices – the parsley and the tarragon.

Next, spice the quinoa grains with the rice vinegar, olive oil, some salt, pepper, nutmeg, the parsley, and the tarragon.

After that, we switch to the red cabbage. Cut the vegetable in thin stripes and marinade it with balsamic vinegar, olive oil, and the honey.

Consecutively, it is time to prepare the salmon.

Mix all spices with the olive oil, sesame seeds, the sugar, and soak the fish in this marinade for as long as you can wait. You can even start the dish the night before by marinating the salmon overnight.

Next, roast or grill the fish for about 15-20 minutes on medium temperature.

Now we can move to the lentils.

After you have soaked the legumes nicely, strain them from the water and wash thoroughly.

Next, place the lentils in a metal pot along with the diced celery roots, the garlic, olive oil, and a little bit of water.

Leave the mixture to stew until the legumes soften.

Next, add the curry, red pepper, and the vegetable broth.

Stir, blend the mixture, and add the vinegar, the soy sauce, and the agave syrup.

Leave it to simmer on low heat for about 30-40 minutes.

Next, puree the lentils with a hand blender.

Now we can start arranging the dish (finally!).

Place a portion of the lentil puree in a plate.

Put 1 salmon filet at the top, sprinkle some marinated red cabbage stripes, and garnish with the quinoa!

Phew! That's it! The only thing left is to enjoy!

My notes:

Chestnut & Squash Cream Soup

Ingredients:

1 average **Butternut squash**
1 cup **Edible chestnuts** (roasted and peeled)
1 large **Onion bulb**
3 stalks **Celery**
3-4 Tbsps. **Butter**
1/2 tsp. **Paprika**
1/2 tsp. **Pepper**
1/4 tsp. **Cayenne pepper**
1/2 tsp. **Cumin**
1/2 tsp. **Savory**
Salt – to taste

Instructions:

First, dice the onion and the celery.

Next, place them in a metal pot with a lid along with the butter and a little bit of water. Seal the pot and let the veggies simmer until they soften.

In the meantime, cut the squash in average cubes and add them to the onion and celery mixture.

Cover the vegetables with some boiling water and put the lid back on so that the pumpkin will be well cooked.

Next, mash (or crush) the chestnuts and add them to the soup. If they are not soft enough – simply cut them in quarters.

Leave the ingredients to simmer and soften for about 30 minutes, and puree them with a hand blender until you reach the desired consistency.

And that's it!

Feel free to decorate the soup when serving with seeds and spices of your choice and preferences.

Vegetable Cream Soup with Croutons

Ingredients:

For the soup:
2 large **Red peppers**
1 large **Onion bulb**
10 cloves **Garlic**
2 large **Potatoes**
2 cups **Cauliflower**
3 **Carrots**
3-4 Tbsps. **Butter**
Some **Olive oil** – to taste
Salt and pepper – to taste

For the croutons:
Some old **Gluten-free bread**
Olive oil
Salt
Paprika

Instructions:

First, dice the peppers and the onion bulb.

Pour some olive oil in a metal pot and add the minced veggies along with the whole peeled garlic cloves.

Add just a little bit of water and seal the pot to let the vegetables stew until soft.

In the meantime, cut the potatoes and the carrots in medium chunks and chop off the cauliflower florets.

Next, add them to the softened onion, peppers, and the garlic, spice the dish with some salt and pepper, and stir for a minute or two.

Consecutively, add more water to fully cover the ingredients, and let them simmer until everything is completely cooked and soft.

After that, simply blend the soup with a hand blender to reach a homogeneous smooth consistency.

Finally, add the butter and stir again.

Now that our soup is ready, we can continue with the croutons.

Heat a skillet, cut the gluten-free bread into small cubes, and place them in the hot utensil.

Pour some olive oil and sprinkle the spices.

Stir fry the croutons until nicely golden and crunchy.

And that's it!

My notes:

Mangold Soup (Vegan)

Ingredients:

1 large bunch of **Mangold** (chard)
1 **Onion bulb**
1 **Carrot**
1 **Tomato**
1 1/2 Tbsp. **Rice**
Salt and fennel – to taste
Some **Olive oil**
Water
Some **Cream cheese** – optional

Instructions:

First, mince the onion, the carrot, and the tomato in small pieces.

Next, heat a metal pot with some oil and cook the veggies until they soften.

Now add the rice, the water, and let the mixture cook for 10 more minutes.

Meanwhile, remove the mangold stems and cut the leaves in thin stripes.

Add the leafy greens to the soup and let it simmer for about 20 minutes.

Finally, spice the dish with some minced fennel and garnish with some cream cheese (or yogurt). If you prefer the soup to be vegan, just skip this step.

Summer Russian Soup (Okroshka)

Ingredients:

2 cups **Yogurt** (or kefir)
1/2 **Cucumber**
1/2 **Carrot**
1 average **Potato** (boiled)
Some **Bacon** (as much as you like)
1 **Boiled egg**
Salt and fennel – to taste
2-3 cloves **Garlic**
Some **Olive oil** (about 3-4 Tbsps.)
Water

Instructions:

This recipe can be changed and tweaked entirely to your taste and preferences. But here are some basic guidelines.

Dice the cucumber, the egg, the garlic cloves, bacon, and the potato.

Grate the carrot or mince it in a kitchen chopper.

Cut the fennel in small pieces as well.

Now blend all ingredients well and add some water to reach the consistency of a soup.

Place the dish in the fridge for 4 hours to develop its taste.

Easy peasy!

Low Carb Summer Bulgarian Soup with Radish (Tarator)

Ingredients:

2 cups **Yogurt** (or kefir)
A bunch of **Radishes**
1/2 cup **Water**
1 clove **Garlic**
1 Tbsp. **Extra virgin olive oil**
1/2 tsp. **Pepper**
1/4 tsp. **Salt** (adjust to taste)

Instructions:

This recipe is very simple and easy to prepare!

Place the yogurt, the water, and the spices in a blender and homogenize the mixture well.

Next, clean the radishes and cut them in small chunks along with the garlic clove.

Transfer the veggies into the blender, add the olive oil, and stir until the soup becomes smooth and homogeneous.

Store in the fridge and stir well before serving!

Easy as that!

My notes:

Red Lentil Pate (Vegan)

Ingredients:

1 cup **Red lentils**
1/2 cup **Dry tomatoes**
1/2 cup **Walnuts**
1/2 cup **Dried olives** (raisin olives)
2 Tbsps. **Extra virgin olive oil**
1/2 tsp. **Cumin**
1 clove **Garlic**
Salt, oregano, and pepper – to taste

Instructions:

First, boil the legumes and let them cool down completely.

Next, if the walnuts are raw, roast them in a dry hot non-stick pan.

Now mince them in a blender.

Next, pit the olives and add them to the ground walnuts along with the tomatoes, the garlic, and the olive oil.

Mince and homogenize the mixture well.

Now strain the lentils and add them to the puree.

Add the spices and the lemon juice and blend again until you reach a nice and smooth consistency (as much as possible).

This is an excellent dip or a side dish!

Thank you!

I want to thank you for purchasing this book and reading it all the way to the end. I hope it has been helpful and informative. If you liked this volume, you can support my work and make it more visible for others who are looking for this kind of knowledge! I would deeply appreciate if you take a minute and write a short review on Amazon. I thank you in advance for your support!
Kind regards and best wishes,
Milica

P.S. And don't forget to get your free ebooks:
"***10 Powerful Immune Boosting Recipes***"
"***12 Healthy Dessert Recipes***"
"***15 Delicious & Healthy Smoothies***"
"***The Complete Ayurveda Detox***"

Go to ***www.MindBodyAndSpiritWellbeing.com*** and claim your gifts!

Or simply scan the QR code below:

About the author

Milica Vladova dedicated her work to spread the valuable knowledge of the physical, emotional, and spiritual wellbeing. She is determined to make the world healthier, happier, and more successful!

Her works have been published on *The Huffington Post*, *Thrive Global*, *The Elephant Journal*, *Sivana Spirit*, *YogiApproved*, *Steven Aitchison*, and more.

Find her on:
http://mindbodyandspiritwellbeing.com
https://facebook.com/**mindbodyandspiritwellbeing**
https://www.pinterest.com/**milicavladova**
https://twitter.com/**Holistic_Milky**

Milica is also the author of:

Easy Gluten Free Desserts

111 IRRESISTIBLE GLUTEN-FREE DESSERT RECIPES

"Easy Gluten Free Desserts" will enchant you with its simple and delicious recipes!
You will find tons of tasty and sweet ideas for your gluten-free lifestyle!

Get ready for:
-> **Healthy pancakes** packed with fiber;
-> **Delicious cakes** and pies without white sugar and artificial sweeteners;
-> Gluten-free **muffins and brownies**;
-> **Tasty cookies** for your tummy and soul;
-> Cheesecakes recipes, terrines, sweet breads,
-> and so much more!

Satisfy your sweet cravings with these simple, yummy, and healthy sweets and dive into the waters of gluten-free cooking with "Easy Gluten Free Desserts"!

Your body will thank you!

The Healthy Vegan Recipes Cookbook

MORE THAN 80 HEALTHY VEGAN RECIPES FOR THE WHOLE FAMILY!

In this volume you will find:
- Healthy vegan **main course dishes**;
- **Bread and salty snacks** recipes.
- **Dips and side dishes**.
- Yummy **sugar-free desserts**.
- Interesting info about **the numerous benefits of vegan foods**. and more!

★★★★★Perfect when you're in a pinch!

I referred to this recipe book several times over the past week to get some healthy, tasty recipes for my vegan/vegetarian friends. The author definitely has first-hand experience preparing these dishes, provides clear tips and alternatives, and also imparts knowledge about the health benefits. I'm short, it's a practical recipe book, but it's also an insightful read. I'll be reaching for this book over the holiday season for more inspiration. I'm thinking of pulling together a raw nut loaf and I'm pretty sure I saw a recipe in here I could swing! I know it won't disappoint! (I'm considering purchasing a hard copy this Xmas for a raw food friend!)

~ Cynthia Luna on Amazon.com

★★★★★Try these recipes!

Lots of wonderful recipes that I cannot wait to try. Healthy and nutritious meals! Snacks!

~ Aisha Hashmi on Amazon.com

Complete Body Cleansing and Strong Immunity Bundle

- **Healthy recipes** with white sugar and white flour alternatives!
- Plenty of toning, refreshing, and cleansing **smoothie recipes**!
- Detoxing and strengthening aromatic **herbal blends**!
- Loads of delicious **immune boosting recipes** and remedies.
- Which exercises can help us **expel more toxins** from our cells;
- **Simple weekly, monthly, and annual detox rituals** to help you boost your energy, lose weight naturally, fight chronic fatigue, and prevent from diseases.
- How to purify your system **without starving**?
- How to **deeply detox and heal your colon, liver, kidneys, lungs, lymph**, and more?
- How to naturally **get rid of parasites**?
- **Healthy gut - healthy you!** How to take care of our beneficial colon bacteria?
- **Natural probiotics and prebiotics** - how to make them at home with natural ingredients?
- **Adaptogens** - the key to dealing with stress, infertility and building our strong immunity.
- Natural ways and systems to **prevent, stop, and heal from cancer** cell formation.
- **The best herbs, essential oils and homeopathic remedies** to prevent from diseases, viruses, fungi, and bacteria.
- and much more!

★★★★★Science mixed with love for a winning combo

What a wealth of information filled with knowledge and innate insight into how the body functions and heals. So many great choices offered. These books are wonderful at dipping into every day for fresh ideas. Just applying some of the knowledge is still so powerful at helping you get fit and healthy from the inside out. Great recipes and full of science mixed with genuine love from the author.

~ Reviewer on Amazon.com

★★★★★Accessible, clear, and gently written

I wish all health books were written this way!

First, Ms. Vladova shares exhaustive information on cleansing and eating well with such a gentle, non-judgemental attitude.

And she meets the reader where they are. For instance, after introducing the Weekly Fasting Day with just tea or Water, Ms. Vladova suggest that if that is too extreme for you at the beginning, you can start with a day of fasting that involves Green Smoothies instead. And if even that is too much, she offers a plan for a day with just rice and apples.

As someone who's never tried any cleanses, her approach was so accessible!

Second, there is NO FLUFF! She gets right into talking about how to eat better and cleanse your body.

Recipes are easy to understand and well explained.

~ J D on Amazon.com

★★★★★ **The Perfect Christmas Stocking Filler - A Recovery Programme for those who Overindulge**

Gosh, this is a must-buy for anyone who cares about their body.

I'd already had some great results from the Healthy Body Cleanse detox programme, but the other two books are an absolute bargain - so full of useful information to keep you on track.

Although it's a great Christmas pressie for those of us who have no willpower in the season of gross overindulgence, it's actually a great regime to follow in the month before to prepare your body for the onslaught.

A win-win either way.

~ FireDancer on Amazon.com

★★★★★★**A great resource!**

What a wonderful resource, so jam-packed with information! The body has a great mechanism to heal itself and these books help with that. I'm really pleased because my daily smoothies are now more interesting with the recipes included. The other recipes are easily adapted if you are vegan like I am. This bundle is what I would term a coffee-table book because once you've read it through you can dip into it every day or whenever you need to be reminded of the great info inside. My health has greatly improved and I recommend this bundle to anyone on the same journey to health or thinking about it.

~ Karen Aminadra on Amazon.com

DIY Homemade Beauty Products Bundle

MORE THAN 500 NATURAL ORGANIC BEAUTY RECIPES FOR THE WHOLE BODY!

What are you going to find in this book?
- Universal **face masks** for all skin types.
- **Lotions and cremes** for oily, dry, and mature skin.
- **Anti-aging and rejuvenating serums** for the face and eye contour.
- Natural **remedies for acne, pimples, blackheads**, etc.
- Gentle **whitening treatments** for brighter complexion and radiant skin.
- Universal nourishing **hair masks**;
- **Hair repair** recipes;
- **Anti-split ends** treatments;
- Natural **remedies for hair-loss** and thinning hair;
- **Hair growth** stimulators;
- **Dandruff healing masks** and ointments for oily and itchy scalp;
- **Herbal rinsing, organic shampoo recipes** and oil blends;
- Nourishing **body butters and lotions**;
- **Non-toxic sunscreen** recipes;
- Cleansing and healing **body scrubs and exfoliators**;
- **Anti-cellulite treatments** and massaging oils;
- Nourishing and **anti-aging hand cremes** and masks;
- **Nail strengthening** procedures;
- Natural **toothpastes and mouthwashes**;
- and more...

★★★★★Great deal!

This budle is a great resource for homemade beauty products! These are gentle and natural products!

~ **Kelly Phister on Amazon.com**

★★★★★**Great set of books that has numerous recipes for everyone**

Great set of books that has numerous recipes for every item.

The ingredients required are not difficult to come by. Overall a very nice and helpful set of books that comes in very handy for lotions and hand creams, hair masks etc. I recommend this book.

~ **Joanne Beal on Amazon.com**

★★★★★**Start saving money and be healthier, too!**

Talk about your natural resource for all things you purchase. Now I am the first one to tell people to stop buying prepare items like soap, shampoo and the like, and to make their own. I go to Lush religiously and purchase their items. It is all natural barring a few essential ingredients that are needed to preserve the products, and even them it is as gentle and natural as possible. Show yourself some love and get this book, and save yourself some money at Lush, because their products are not cheap and this DIY boom is loaded with so much and really is worth the small price investment as you will save literally thousands with all these recipes and all the imformation!

~ **Aisha Hashmi on Amazon.com**

Printed in Great Britain
by Amazon